PRAISE FOR
MAKE YOUR DESTINY HAPPEN

"This is more than a book—it's a call to action for anyone ready to break free from limitation and take command of their future. With vulnerability, wisdom, and purpose, the author reveals a transformational model that empowers you to rise after failure, find clarity in chaos, and design a destiny that's truly your own. Let this be your blueprint for a life of meaning, momentum, and mastery."

—**Ken Morris, Founder & CEO KnectIQ Inc.**

"Leggett's Destiny Development Delta Model is transformational genius in action. His framework doesn't just inspire—it equips readers with practical tools to break free from the cycle of no destiny control. This book articulates what I've observed throughout my career: true leadership begins with leading yourself. An essential read for anyone serious about authoring their own "success to significance" destiny."

—**Khwaja Shaik, CTO, Industry Market, IBM**

"Donzel Leggett is a transformational leader so he understands what it takes to create meaningful transformation—in business and in life. His approach is grounded, practical, and deeply inspiring. The results of his leadership are visible and impactful."

—**Sylvia Wulf, Board Chair AquaBounty Technologies Inc.**

"Through relatable stories, and a clearly articulated system, Donzel Leggett has created a powerful guide that is understandable, motivating and actionable. This book offers readers the tools and mindset to take charge of their lives and careers—at any stage—and to drive to the outcomes they seek."

—**Susan Yashur, Retired Deloitte Global Deputy CEO and General Counsel**

"I've had the pleasure of knowing Donzel for over 15 years, and this book is a powerful reflection of the passion, clarity, and purpose he brings to everything he does. *Make Your Destiny Happen* is both inspiring and practical—a deeply personal roadmap to transformation rooted in lived experience and hard-earned wisdom. The Destiny Development Delta model is a timely and energizing guide for anyone ready to take control of their path and define success on their own terms."

—Cheryl Bethune, Global HR Executive

"We are going through very challenging times in the world which also means opportunity. If we create awareness for our own values, aspirations, have a plan, it is much easier to adapt, learn and proceed. I definitely enjoyed and found similarities in our approach to life and how we work with a plan in Donzel Leggett's book which reminded me one more time how authenticity is important in our daily approaches and thoughtful plans."

—Umran Beba, August Leadership, Partner; Beba Foundation, Co- Founder; and Independent Board Director, Bakkavor

"Donzel Leggett, after decades of life experiences and leadership roles at a Fortune 500 company, understands the importance of planning for success. *Make Your Destiny Happen* is a must-read for anyone wanting to take control of their life."

—Peter Cook, Managing Director, Investments

"I have known Donzel for years, and have had the opportunity to see him in action. In both the for-profit and not-for-profit worlds. His actions and his words always leave me inspired. I'm confident you will enjoy his words as you craft and chase your dreams."

—Jeff Prouty, Chairman and Founder at The Prouty Project Inc.

"Donzel's story of overcoming struggles through authentic positivity & modeled behavior is not only inspirational, but very relatable, as the parallels are rich to our very own storied lives. Thank you, Donzel, for continuing to remind us all, that much of our lives, really are in our own hands."

—**Ari Zainuddin, Chief Purpose Officer am__+ brands**

MAKE YOUR DESTINY HAPPEN

Take Control of Your Life with the
Destiny Development Delta Model
for Transformational Success

DONZEL A. LEGGETT

Copyright © 2025 by Donzel A. Leggett

Destiny Development Delta™, iLEAD Change™, A-Attitudes of Leadership™, and Make Your Destiny Happen™ are registered trademarks of Destiny Development Delta LLC.

All rights reserved.

First edition published August 2025

ISBNs: 979-8-9929806-1-5 (hardcover), 979-8-9929806-2-2 (eBook)

Unless otherwise noted, all quotes have been provided courtesy of BrainyQuote.com, QuoteFancy.com, GraciousQuotes.com, Goodreads.com, InspiringQuotes.us, and QuoteTab.com.

Graphics by Arthur C. Kegel, Chris Kegel Design LLC

This book is dedicated to all my family and friends who have supported me throughout my life. I could not have done this without you. Thank you for your love.

CONTENTS

1. **INTRODUCTION** — 1

2. **DESTINY DEVELOPMENT DELTA MODEL BACKGROUND** — 7
   - **Chapter 1:** Main Messages of Section 2 — 9
   - **Chapter 2:** My Story and the Origins of the Destiny Development Delta Model — 11
   - **Chapter 3:** The Activation of My Life Plan — 17
   - **Chapter 4:** Why Is the Feeling of Controlling One's Destiny So Important? — 25
   - **Chapter 5:** The Importance of Understanding Transformation Versus Change — 37

3. **DESTINY DEVELOPMENT DELTA MODEL OVERVIEW** — 47
   - **Chapter 6:** Main Messages of Section 3 — 49
   - **Chapter 7:** Destiny Development Delta Model Introduction — 51
   - **Chapter 8:** Destiny Development Delta Integrated Model Overview — 55
   - **Chapter 9:** The Three Major Milestones of the Destiny Development Delta Model Deployment Process — 59

4. **MILESTONE 1: THE A-ATTITUDES OF LEADERSHIP MODEL** — 63
   - **Chapter 10:** Main Messages of Section 4 — 65
   - **Chapter 11:** The A-Attitudes of Leadership Model — 67
   - **Chapter 12:** The A-Attitudes of Leadership Foundational Tier — 69
   - **Chapter 13:** The A-Attitudes of Leadership Intrapersonal Tier — 81
   - **Chapter 14:** The A-Attitudes of Leadership Interpersonal Tier — 89

Chapter 15: The A-Attitudes of Leadership Apex Tier	101
Chapter 16: The A-Attitudes of Leadership Development Models and Processes	109
Chapter 17: Holistic Balance and Personal Well-Being Development	115
Chapter 18: The A-Attitudes of Leadership Personal Transformation Self-Assessment	121

5. MILESTONE 2: THE iLEAD CHANGE MODEL   125

Chapter 19: Main Messages of Section 5	127
Chapter 20: The iLEAD Change Model	129
Chapter 21: The iLEAD Change Model: Inspire	133
Chapter 22: The iLEAD Change Model: Light	153
Chapter 23: The iLEAD Change Model: Engage	165
Chapter 24: The iLEAD Change Model: Activate	181
Chapter 25: The iLEAD Change Model: Develop	201

6. MILESTONE 3: THE FORMULA FOR SUCCESS   223

Chapter 26: Main Messages of Section 6	225
Chapter 27: The Formula for Success	227

7. CLOSE AND CALL TO ACTION   237

Chapter 28: Call to Action	239

8. ABOUT THE AUTHOR AND DESTINY DEVELOPMENT DELTA LLC   241

SECTION 1

INTRODUCTION

INTRODUCTION

Do you want to make your destiny happen?

In 1993, when I was twenty-four years old, I asked myself that same question. I decided that my answer was yes and developed a life plan that laid the road map for my journey to take control of my life and my destiny. Since that time, I have been steadily advancing that life plan for my family, career, financial stability, community, and, most importantly, authentic happiness. It is gratifying knowing that I am activating *my plan*, the plan that I developed to take me where I want to go. My plan to achieve the destiny and legacy that I desire for myself, not the one that others want for me. Just having a plan is critically important to my personal well-being, now more than ever, in a world that is chaotic and overwhelming at times and that creates unprecedented stress, discontent, and feelings of insignificance and depression for many.

There is no question that I have been fortunate in my life and that I have had a lot of help and support along the way, but I have also had to overcome some of the same struggles and challenges that many of you have.

I've QUIT.

I've FAILED.

I've LOST.

I have had setbacks and faced obstacles that have challenged my self-confidence and drive and that have made me wonder, *Am I good enough? Do I have what it takes?* I have experienced fear and uncertainty that made me ask myself, *What if I'm wrong? What if I make a mistake?*

Over the course of my journey, I have learned many valuable lessons that helped me overcome these challenges. From these lessons, I developed several support models, processes, and tools to ultimately help me persevere, succeed, and win. I have integrated this knowledge into the Destiny Development Delta model for transformational success.

Because of the Destiny Development Delta model, I wake up every morning inspired to start a new day and to further advance my journey to make my destiny happen. I am energized to keep moving my plan forward and to turn challenges and setbacks into opportunities to learn and grow. I feel a positive energy propelling me physically, mentally, and spiritually not only to advance my destiny plan but also to help others transform and achieve their life goals. For me, success and legacy include helping you make your destiny happen and leaving a positive and sustaining impact on society.

As you read this book, it is important to note that when I refer to your destiny, it is not what others want for you but what you want for yourself. You define what success and legacy are for you. I can tell you that having the clarity of knowing what you want for yourself and being in control of your life and destiny are wonderfully fulfilling and energizing feelings, and I want to inspire and enable you to experience that as well by sharing my personal story of transformation and the Destiny Development Delta model.

In this book, I will do the following:

- Introduce the Destiny Development Delta model for transformational success and illustrate how and why it is uniquely suited to help you make your destiny happen.
- Provide an in-depth explanation of the two main components of the model: the A-attitudes of leadership and the iLEAD change capabilities.
- Share personal stories and examples to bring it all to life.

The book is structured to be easily navigated and to best support your reading style and development. Section 2 identifies the model's origins intertwined with my personal story. In section 3, I provide an overview of the model and explain its integrated components. Sections 4 through 7 are dedicated to a detailed explanation of the deployment of the model. Examples and personal stories are woven throughout the book for real-life relevance. This structure allows you to read front to back or to skip from section to section if that's your preference. I have also included some exercises and reflections to maximize your learning and introduce a little fun.

In summary, I will show you that you can take control of your life and make your destiny happen.

I have quit, but I am a TENACIOUS PERSEVERER.

I have failed, but I am SUCCESSFUL.

I have lost, but I am a WINNER.

I am confident that after reading this book, you will believe in my vision that you can transform your life and control your destiny by committing to the Destiny Development Delta model.

Congratulations on taking the first step!

SECTION 2
DESTINY DEVELOPMENT DELTA MODEL BACKGROUND

CHAPTER 1

MAIN MESSAGES OF SECTION 2

The purpose of this section is to provide the background and context that led to the creation of the Destiny Development Delta model. In section 2, I will do the following:

- Share the important events and relevant stories that birthed my life plan, which drove the creation, over many years, of what would become the basis for the Destiny Development Delta model and are critical to explaining its origin.
- Describe the activation of my life plan, highlight the results, and explain major adjustments made to successfully navigate significant life and family changes, as well as unprecedented environmental and societal factors, while staying true to myself.
- Explain why it is more important than ever for every person to feel that they can lead and build the capability to control their destiny. You are the leader of your life, and to control your destiny, you must start to see yourself as a leader.
- Introduce the cycle of no destiny control model to clearly illustrate and explain the pattern in which many people are trapped, preventing them from taking control of their lives and destinies, and discuss what it takes to break out of this cycle.
- Introduce change and transformation, define them both, and clearly articulate the difference between the two.
- Explain why the Destiny Development Delta model is best suited to help you escape the cycle of no destiny control and embrace transformation.

CHAPTER 2

MY STORY AND THE ORIGINS OF THE DESTINY DEVELOPMENT DELTA MODEL

I am originally from Key West, Florida, the southernmost point of the continental United States. Key West is a very unique place that attracts many visitors from all over the world and is home to a highly diverse population with many interesting characters. If you have ever been there, you know what I am talking about. Growing up in Key West taught me to respect differences and to value all people, no matter their appearance, sexual orientation, or lifestyle. I learned early on that one should never judge a book by its cover, only by its contents.

The majority of my family immigrated from the Bahamas in the mid 1800s. My history is shaped by very strong women who were the leaders of our family. My great-grandmother was a wet nurse, which means that her job was to breastfeed other people's children, exclusively wealthy white people's. It is ironic that, as a Black woman, she was entrusted to breastfeed their babies, but they didn't value her enough to allow her to enter their homes through their front doors. My grandmother was a maid. Her knees and elbows were always dark and calloused from hand-scrubbing floors because she took pride in her work and wanted it done right. Neither of them received more than a sixth-grade education. But they had tremendous self-worth and incredible strength, courage, and faith. They sacrificed so that their children and future generations would have opportunities for better lives through hard work and education.

My parents were married for almost seventy years and lived their entire lives in Key West. My father worked at Southern Bell, and later Bell South, for forty-three years and was a proud member of the

Communication Workers of America. He started out as a janitor and worked his way up to a linesman, the technicians who drive the big cherry-picker trucks. He taught me perseverance and hard work. My mother worked for the United States Navy Civil Service for almost twenty years, then served as executive director for a preschool for another twenty years. She has been a recognized leader in the community for more than fifty years, regularly sought out to speak and sing at important events and to serve on committees and boards in the city and in Monroe County. She taught me to always help others, to be accountable, and to never betray my values and character, even when faced with tough choices.

My mother prioritized the value of education, and because of this I stayed focused on being a very good student. My academic record, coupled with the fact that I was six feet five inches tall and weighed 225 pounds at sixteen, earned me a full athletic scholarship to study at Purdue University in West Lafayette, Indiana, and to play in the prestigious Big Ten Conference. My goal at Purdue was to be a role model student-athlete. And that's what I did. I started more than twenty games as defensive end for the Boilermakers. I earned Academic All-Big Ten honors three times and Academic All-America honors in 1988. I did well individually, but my team did not.

I later realized that sometimes it's not enough to be just a good role model. Sometimes a leader has to step up and do more, and I simply didn't do enough. It's not about what you think the team needs; it's about what the team actually needs. I reflected on who I was and who I wanted to be and realized that leadership was something I identified with and was good at, but I had the self-insight to recognize that I had some work to do to fully understand and appreciate how far I wanted to go and what I was willing to sacrifice.

After graduating in 1990 with a Bachelor of Science and taking a semester off, I returned to Purdue to pursue a Master of Science in industrial technology. It was during my second tenure at Purdue that I met my future wife, Tracy. She graduated with a Bachelor of Arts in the spring of 1992 and shortly thereafter became pregnant, which triggered the beginning of my transformation and the development of my initial life plan.

After earning my master's degree in December 1992, I was hired as an industrial engineer by a large US-based food manufacturing company. One and a half years later, Tracy and I were married and expecting our second child. I was on track to realizing a successful engineering career, with two promotions under my belt, and felt like things were going well. However, the situation changed quickly, and I made an unplanned move into management. How that happened was the first clear indication I had of the type of leader I could be and how it would influence my life plan.

I was working at the company's flagship factory, which was one of the largest in the world at that time. The facility was more than one hundred years old and employed about eleven hundred people, many second- and third-generation employees. All of the hourly employees were represented by trade unions, and the company had a history of management and union conflict. People-of-color diversity represented fewer than 1 percent of the population, and there had been only one female and one person of color in operations management in its history. The factory was also not performing well at the time and labor relations were once again rocky. But even in this environment, I loved my engineering job because it gave me the opportunity to spend all my time on the production shop floor building relationships and finding ways to make people's jobs safer and easier while also improving the plant's performance.

The production department manager abruptly left the company, and a new manager was needed urgently. This was a high-profile and sought-after job, and most thought it would go to an established manager from another factory with seven to ten years of proven leadership experience in large union environments. I didn't even consider inquiring about it because I loved being an engineer and didn't want the job and because I didn't think that I was anywhere near qualified, since I was fewer than two years removed from college with no management experience.

Unbeknownst to me, the department employees went to the union president and asked him to tell the plant manager that if he wanted to improve labor relations, he should make me the new manager because I was the only one who cared about and listened to them. The plant manager called me and explained what was happening, then asked me to interview for the job. I was shocked, to say the least, and told him that I was not interested, nor did I think I was ready for the position. He explained that he had given his word to the union president that he would offer me an interview. I told him again that I wasn't sure I wanted to do that. Besides loving my engineering job, as a twenty-five-year-old recent college graduate, I didn't relish managing several hundred people more than twice my age. He asked if I would at least think about it and let him know the next day. I said I would, but I was still leaning heavily against interviewing.

My initial life plan called for me to move into management within the next five years, but I had not planned on it being in operations and certainly not in this plant and for the department in which I had been trained. I simply didn't think it was the right time, place, or situation. That evening, I asked one of my best friends at the plant, who was also a union employee, for his advice. He said, "Donzel, I heard about the petition to make you the manager, but I stayed out of it so that no one could say I influenced it because I'm your friend. But here's what I can tell you. You're an excellent engineer, and everyone knows that. But more importantly, you demonstrate character, and you genuinely care for and help people. You inspire others to want to do more because you engage everyone as if they each matter. Again, you're a great engineer, but we need a leader. The people here see you as that leader, and we need you to step up and lead us now. So take the interview, get the job, and have no regrets."

From that moment, I knew that I was on the right track with my life plan. I understood that controlling my destiny would mean always being prepared for the unexpected and being ready to make tough decisions to take advantage of opportunities when they present themselves. I learned that it was OK, and in fact necessary, to adjust my plan if I stay in control. In this case, I recognized that I could accelerate my career and life goals while also making a difference in people's lives. I took the interview, got the job, and haven't had any regrets.

Fast-forward to today, and my original life plan that led to the Destiny Development Delta model has allowed me to achieve what I call successes regarding family, career, and community impact. I am striving to be the best and controlling my destiny, just as I envisioned it almost thirty years ago. I wrote this book to provide you with the inspiration and capability to achieve the destiny that you desire and deserve.

CHAPTER 3

THE ACTIVATION OF MY LIFE PLAN

The first section of my initial life plan was the most important—establishing a strong, stable, and loving family unit. I married my girlfriend while she was pregnant with our second child, and we have had a happy marriage that is now in its thirty-first year. We have raised four children, one son and three daughters, and they have all grown into wonderful adults. They all are doing well, and we are so very proud of them. They are all university graduates and gainfully employed (and off my payroll). They are all still young and early in their life journey, but they are driven to be successful in the career paths of their choosing. Most importantly, they are all great people with outstanding interpersonal skills, emotional intelligence, well-being, and judgment, and they say that this is because of how they were raised.

Each of our children has always been willing to stand up for those whom others would marginalize. And each sees themselves as world citizens and treats all people with the respect with which that person would want to be treated (the platinum rule). They were raised through some of the most incredible and life-changing advancements in the last fifty years, to include the advent of the information age, social media, and artificial intelligence. But they've also lived through some of the most tumultuous and divisive events, including climate change, the COVID-19 pandemic, wars, geopolitical instability, social unrest, and intense political tribalism. And yet they have all remained hopeful and engaged in their own ways to stand up for what is right and for those unable to stand up for themselves. As parents, we wanted to be present and to raise our kids to be leaders; to have strength, perseverance, and adaptability; to develop the academic and social skills to be successful in whatever career they chose; and, above all else, to truly be good people. There is no doubt we have achieved this.

I felt it was critical for me to focus on establishing the foundation for a strong and happy family by being the very *best husband* I could be and partnering with my wife to be the *best parents* we could be by providing a stable and loving home for our kids. But being the *best father* is more than that, so I prioritized life-work balance to ensure my physical, mental, and emotional presence as a dad. I would strive to be at every school event, help with homework, bathe and clothe the kids, read bedtime stories, and even style my daughters' hair (much to their chagrin) every night that I could. I planned to coach them in sports, support their interests, and do all the things that best nurture kids and that make families as close and as happy as any in the world. I planned to ensure that my kids would never feel like or say, "I don't really know my dad" or "My dad was not there." Both my wife and I believe that we delivered on our goals of being great parents, building a caring and loving home, and raising four wonderful young people. We are controlling our destinies as a family.

The next section of my initial life plan was focused on setting and accomplishing my career goals, which were to become a C-suite executive in a Fortune 500 company (one of the largest companies in the United States), then, after retiring from corporate America, to start my own business and run for United States Congress. Over the course of my thirty-two years in corporate life, I feel that I have had a truly outstanding career and have achieved my career life goals. I always strived to be the best leader, continuously developed myself, and authentically led by putting people first. I generated tremendous results in all my roles, created a climate that allowed all people to succeed, and always did it the right way. I earned the reputation of a great leader, one who both drives unparalleled performance and stands up for his people and always has their backs.

I was determined that nothing would stop me from achieving my life goals, so I earned my MBA, my second master's degree, and learned not only Spanish (which was in my original life plan) but also Portuguese.

If there was a glass ceiling, I was going to shatter it by being so good that there was no way I could be denied. And I was going to do it by being authentically me. I started my career as an associate industrial engineer in training and finished it after eleven promotions as a vice president with global accountabilities. Over the last sixteen years of my career, I worked internationally and have proven that my unique ability to lead by putting people first translates across geographies, languages, and cultures. I have traveled the world and built tremendous relationships with friends in Brazil, Mexico, China, India, France, Greece, Spain, the United Kingdom, South Korea, Singapore, Taiwan, Australia, New Zealand, the UAE, and Saudi Arabia, just to name a few. All of this was part of my initial life plan from a career perspective, and I have moved on to the next phase of launching my own company with Destiny Development Delta LLC.

The next section of my initial life plan was to establish financial stability to take care of my immediate family, help my extended family, and allow the flexibility to support causes in the community to positively impact the lives of others. Through thrifty spending, disciplined saving, and actively managing my investments, we have been able to meet our financial stability and wealth creation goals. Money did not buy my happiness. Instead, focusing on being the best husband, father, son, family member, and community citizen has. However, it's important to note that financial security and flexibility have made a difference in our quality of life and what we were able to provide our children.

With that said, I am most proud of the things I have been able to do for my extended family. At the top of the list was buying my parents a new home. My mother and father had owned their own home since 1979, but they had a small lot in the middle of a densely populated block. The house also had limited space for family gatherings and a cramped kitchen that made it tough to prepare big meals and comfortably dine together. The neighborhood was also becoming crowded with increasingly dubious activity, noise at night, and nowhere to park. On top of all that, there was still a mortgage on the home, which required my mom to continue working at seventy-nine years old. I wanted my mother to finally retire for good, but I knew that the only way to do that was to eliminate the burden of that mortgage.

I told my mom to sell their house and keep the profit and that I would buy them a brand-new home on a larger lot with more space to entertain. The new home also had a bigger kitchen, lots of parking, the safety of a gated community, and her very own ocean view and boat dock in her backyard. Owning oceanfront property in Key West is extremely rare, and I don't know anyone in our family who ever has. To be able to provide this for my parents on the island on which they were born and raised and where our family has lived for four generations was an incredibly awesome accomplishment and still gives me goose bumps to this day. I don't know about other cultures, but many little African American boys dream of buying their mom a new house when they grow up by becoming a professional athlete or performer or by doing whatever it takes on the streets to make the necessary money. I was able to accomplish this dream by following my life plan to successfully navigate my career and build the financial stability and wealth to enable it.

I was also able to buy and completely renovate my grandmother's home. My grandparents purchased this home in 1965 by saving every single penny they earned as a maid and a construction laborer, an incredible feat at that time. But the home had fallen into some degree of disrepair over the years, and the family was faced with the decision of either investing a large sum of money into fixing it or selling it, which they did not want to do because it would mean that the one thing my grandmother left for her descendants would no longer be in the family. Because of my life plan, I was able to remove a financial burden from my family while also honoring my grandparents by buying the home and fully remodeling it. I know my grandmother would be so very proud.

Financial stability has also provided us the flexibility to support causes in the community to positively impact the lives of others. My wife has been able to be a full-time volunteer and community organizer most of our married lives, directly influencing such causes as K–12 education, government elections, school district bonding bills, and important social issue votes combating racism, hate, and other forms of marginalization like poverty and homelessness. Community organizing, motivating, and facilitating people to drive positive social change is her life passion, and she is really good at it. The activation of my life plan has enabled her to pursue her passion, control her destiny, and positively impact others.

In 2018, I decided to run for public office because many people were concerned about the lack of moral leadership in politics and asked me to run to inspire hope and faith in leadership. This was not a part of my plan at this stage of my life, but as I mentioned, an important component of the Destiny Development Delta model is that the plan be alive and adaptable because circumstances change, requiring you to sometimes call an audible or change in direction. Making this adjustment to my plan meant that, win or lose, my career trajectory in corporate America, as well as my future income, would take a significant hit, but because I was self-assured and had followed my life plan to build financial stability, I was able to make this decision, stand up for what I believed in, and do what was right for my community. With my wife as my campaign manager, I ran on a platform of leadership over politics and representation for all, and we reignited hope in thousands of people. I was able to inspire almost 20 percent of those who had voted the other way in the prior election to change their preference and vote for me. We came within a half of a percent, or 116 votes, of winning in a district thought impossible for us to even be competitive in. We lost, but the growth that my wife and I experienced, the friendships we made, and, most importantly, the knowledge that we were doing the right thing and authentically inspiring people as we did it was an awesome feeling. The decision to run for office stalled my career, and I failed to achieve my objective of reaching the C-suite, costing me at least $5 million, and I lost the election. I failed, I lost at a big cost, and I lost again. But I still controlled my destiny.

As I mentioned earlier, having a life plan that is centered and authentic provides the foundation from which you can quickly pivot and seamlessly adjust during times of unpredictable and unprecedented change when tough decisions must be made, when it is hard to know what to do and how to keep yourself inspired and moving forward. This is why understanding that flexibility is important and has been critical to my successful life plan navigation. Because I had done the work of authentically knowing myself, what my values were, and what I wanted out of life and built a plan to structurally bring it all to fruition, I was always prepared when unforeseen and unprecedented issues and crises arose.

When the COVID-19 pandemic first occurred and countries around the world began to mandate lockdown orders, many people did not know what to do or how to handle this sudden change from a career management standpoint. Because I had a fully developed life plan, I was able to quickly adapt and adjust. It is important to remember that we are all in different situations. Depending on their field and level of work, some people were affected more significantly than others and may not have had the resources and support that I had. Many were laid off temporarily, furloughed, or terminated because their business or because the business for which they worked couldn't survive. This is why everyone needs to build their own specific life plan tailored to their circumstances that allows for adjustments and pivots and that considers contingencies in anticipation of unforeseen issues. In other words, you need to have a backup plan for the backup plan when crap unexpectedly happens.

For me, I had specified in my life plan that five years from that time, I would write a book and start my own business with global reach. When the pandemic stay-at-home orders became clear, I immediately adjusted my plan to move up these milestones to take advantage of the additional discretionary time at home, since I wouldn't be traveling, commuting, going out for dinner or shopping, or having my time wasted with non-value-added meetings. I wrote my business plan, formed my limited liability company, wrote this book, and developed my specific coaching program along with all the associated support materials.

I also refreshed and expanded my multilingual capability and increased my knowledge of world cultures and history through study and research. I refined the skills and processes in distance leadership that I had developed from having geographically dispersed teams over the prior twenty-one years to virtually build relationships, drive connections, and effectively coach across countries, cultures, and time zones. I worked to improve these processes in preparation for ensuring that my influence would be best suited for the new post-pandemic world of increased virtual connection, providing greater flexibility and connectivity, distance learning, and global accessibility.

If you do the work to get to know yourself and what you want authentically, have a centered plan that you are inspired by and believe in, and actively work on your plan and consider contingencies in anticipation of environmental and/or personal changes, you will put yourself in a better position to thrive while others struggle during these tumultuous times.

The point here is not to glorify or celebrate what I have done. Rather, it is to illustrate that because I had the clarity that came from having done the hard work of truly getting to know myself, who I am, what I value, and what I wanted my destiny to be, and because I had a structured yet adaptable life plan, I was able to make the best decisions for my family and for myself. I was able to successfully navigate through some unforeseen changes and unprecedented challenges while staying on track with my objectives and, most importantly, staying true to myself.

I have shared with you how I built and activated my life plan and controlled my destiny. I wrote this book to provide you with the same opportunity by teaching you how to create and initiate your life plan and to make your destiny happen.

CHAPTER 4

WHY IS THE FEELING OF CONTROLLING ONE'S DESTINY SO IMPORTANT?

Earlier, I referenced how changes in my life led to the creation of my life plan and ultimately the Destiny Development Delta model. At that time, I experienced a dramatic moment of clarity that triggered me to look deep inside myself, transform, and establish a new direction. Maybe it was the fact that several pressure points were converging on me at the right time to allow that clarity, conviction, and decisiveness. I was just finishing up my Master of Science degree at Purdue University and had to find a job in the middle of a recession. My family, friends, and mentors had high expectations that I would do something great, but their definition of what that meant varied significantly from one another's ideas and from mine. I had to plan for the reality of my girlfriend's unexpected pregnancy and pay off my college debts. Whatever the reason, it happened. But it doesn't happen this way for most people.

The average person today is dealing not only with their own personal struggles but also with the pressures of a chaotic and overwhelming world. It is very difficult to see clearly with so much noise and debris everywhere, all the time. In 1992, there were societal issues and world crises but nothing like the current environment. The advent of the internet and social media has made the world smaller, allowed people on different continents to connect in real time, and provided every person access to essentially all the information amassed throughout history within seconds. It has also provided a global audience, at virtually no cost, to allow people to rise from obscurity and become influencers.

But at the same time, it has created so many more ways to make people feel small, insignificant, and bullied. The almost infinite amount of content coupled with the widespread use of generative AI, bots, and deepfakes to proliferate misinformation is like an abyss that can drown a person in despair. Then there are those who feel so much pressure to be noticed and gain followers that they spend all their time and creative energy on social media posts, falsely gauging their self-worth by the number of reactions, likes, and followers they receive. And then there are the trolls who use the impersonal and anonymous nature of social media to exploit other people's insecurities with negative comments and destructive and cruel attacks that reinforce their feelings of insignificance, low self-worth, and despair.

The cost of living continues to outpace wages, increasing the percentage of people trapped in practical poverty. The dream of owning a home seems impossible for many, and even investing in oneself with higher education has become an unfortunate trade-off of personal growth for decades of crippling debt. Geopolitically, the dangerous rise of populism continues while two wars threaten global stability. And then there is the increasingly irreversible negative effects of climate change. Considering all this, it's not hard to understand why so many may feel lost, depressed, and powerless or simply not in control of their lives and destinies.

Whether you're a boomer, Gen-Xer, millennial, Zoomer, or Gen Alpha, you might feel the frustration of having life happen *to you* instead of making life happen *for you.* When you make life happen for yourself, you have clear goals, a plan, and a positive outlook of hope to inspire you to move forward through all the craziness and turbulence. But when life is happening to you, it's hard to have the clarity of future goals and plans. If you do have a plan, it's difficult to stay inspired and focused on activating it because of all the distractions, noise, and negative messages that reinforce the thought that it doesn't matter what you do because everything is stacked against you. You lose hope because it feels like an empty promise. You feel like you're stuck in place, a sinking hole that you can't imagine how to break out of. You feel like you're trapped in a cycle of no destiny control.

TRANSFORM TO CONTROL YOUR DESTINY

To make your destiny happen, you will need to transform to be able to recognize, avoid, and escape the cycle of no destiny control. Some of you may be consciously or subconsciously trapped in the cycle right now while others are not but could easily fall into it. Recognizing the cycle and determining whether you are in it is important because all efforts to take control of your destiny will more than likely be fruitless unless you break free.

The cycle of no destiny control has three categories representing the varying levels of nonexistent or inadequate plans to control one's destiny and, relatedly, the lack of hope or belief that one can make it happen. To confidently take control of your destiny, you must have a plan, but you must also have belief in yourself to make your plan happen. Hope without a plan and a plan without hope means you are leaving yourself *to chance*. No plan and no hope gives you *no chance*.

What follows is an explanation of the cycle of no destiny control, how to escape it, and how to transform to control your destiny, including an infographic and a personal story to bring it to life.

First is the flywheel hamster, which represents those people who have a fake plan resulting in fake hope. This group has identified goals and developed a plan, but their goals are not genuine; thus, their plan lacks clear self-insight and commitment. Or because they are inauthentic, their plan is superficial and self-defeating. Or if they have a good plan, they lack the focus and discipline to consistently execute it because they are not inspired, as their goals are not authentically theirs. This results in action with no clear direction and resolve, leading to meandering and inconsistent progress in their lives. In other words, they are going in circles like a hamster on a flywheel. They are on a perpetual spinning treadmill of life, running in place nonstop but going nowhere. They start and stop and go around and around, never moving forward on a consistent basis, thus ending up in the same place they began. By running in place, they trick themselves into believing that they are doing something productive while minimizing risk by ensuring the certainty of their destination, which is the same as where they started. Because they never address the core issue of not having an authentic life plan and therefore hope in that plan, they don't understand why they are not making real and fulfilling progress. They resort to the easiest fix in their mind, which is to change their plan, restart the cycle, and keep the circular flywheel going, re-creating the continued illusion that they are moving forward.

Second is the floating dandelion, which represents those with no plan and misguided hope. This group doesn't have a plan of their own, quite possibly because the self-insight required to push them to identify a goal is hard and feels too much like a commitment; if they don't achieve it, they will be a failure. Instead of setting their own goals and their own path, they hope that they end up on the right path. They hope that things will work out by allowing circumstances to determine what to do, taking advice from their friends, following in the footsteps of their parents, or even copying what they see or read on whatever form of media they interacted with that day. Whatever sounds good and seems easier is the path for them. They tend to change paths frequently and quickly. These decisions are not based on logic or adjustments to environmental changes but on whatever new and interesting concept or direction comes their way. They aimlessly move around and decide in which direction to go based on what others tell them or on the random opportunities that drop into their lap. Their hope is that good fortune or luck will allow them to end up in a fortuitous destination or circumstance. In other words, they are like a dandelion seed floating around on a random path that is determined by whichever direction the wind is blowing at that moment. They will end up somewhere, but their destination is a gamble, pretty much in the hands of chance.

Third is the head-in-the-sand ostrich, which represents those with no hope, so a plan doesn't matter. This group may or may not have identified goals and may or may not have developed a plan, but they are so paralyzed by fear (of failure, success, or the unknown) or apathy ("it doesn't matter what I do anyway" or "everything is stacked against me") that they simply don't do anything. They just keep their head down, take limited to no action, and dream of a lightning strike of good fortune hitting them and changing their life, like winning the lottery. This is, again, quite possibly because they didn't take the time to develop the depth of self-insight to truly determine and lock into their authentic aspirations and/or build the self-assuredness to know that in committing to their dreams, they could overcome the risks and challenges to make it happen. Unlike the flywheel hamster and the floating dandelion, who at least take the risk of trying something and believing it might work, this group doesn't have the hope, the belief, or the assuredness to take the risk of moving at all, but they will fool themselves into thinking that by staying put and playing it safe, they are protecting their destiny. In other words, they are like the ostrich with its head in the sand, going nowhere and oblivious to the fact that the world is passing them by. It's ironic, because by fearing that they will fail and/or thinking that they can't make a difference anyway, they don't act, and by not acting, they don't move forward, which in turn reinforces that they can't make a difference. By keeping their heads in the sand, they blind themselves to this reality so that they can feel safe, but in so doing, they sacrifice the ability to take control of their lives and their destiny.

The solution is to transform to control your destiny. Transforming yourself with the Destiny Development Delta model to have a real plan *plus* real hope will break the cycle of no destiny control and allow you to begin to truly make your destiny happen. With the Destiny Development Delta transformation, you will now be able to replace hope without a plan and a plan with no hope, which is giving yourself *to chance*, and no plan with no hope, which is giving yourself *no chance*, with authentic plan plus authentic hope, which is *assured belief.* Without authentic transformation, people tend to move between the three categories of the cycle, but they never completely break out of it. You can escape the cycle because the authentic self-insight and assured hope developed through the Destiny Development Delta model will provide the leadership, resolve, and commitment to build a comprehensive life plan and hold yourself accountable to take action with consistency and determination over the long term to make your destiny happen. It's like the fifty-year S&P 500 chart—you will have peaks and valleys, but the overall direction of your life will be trending up toward your desired destiny. This is what differentiates the Destiny Development Delta model from other programs. It's an authentic personal transformation and creation of sustained activation of your assured life plan that avoids or breaks you out of the cycle and yields the legacy results that you define. It's also important to note that you must be the leader of your destiny, and it doesn't matter whether you are a leader or manager in your job or career or whether you work inside the home or you are a student, an artist, a cashier, or in any other profession. You should always see yourself as the leader of your life with the power to control your destiny. This is so critical that I will repeat it: you are the leader of your life, and to control your destiny, you must start to see yourself as a leader.

FIGURE 4.1: TRANSFORM TO CONTROL YOUR DESTINY

MY STORY OF BREAKING THE CYCLE OF NO DESTINY CONTROL

The ten most transformative years of my life came between the ages of nineteen and twenty-nine, when many of my most impactful experiences drove my transformation to who I am today. This was the time frame when I built my life plan, and as I mentioned earlier, the key triggering factor for that plan was my girlfriend's unplanned pregnancy and the impending birth of our son. But there were a couple of other experiences prior to this that started the change in my self-insight that would lead to my transformation. One is when I decided to quit college football.

Actually, this was the second time I quit football. The first was during my junior year of high school. Luckily for me, my head coach came to my house and convinced me to return. I did go back, understanding that football was the surest bet for me to attend a great university without my parents bearing the financial burden. A year later I accepted a full athletic scholarship to play football at Purdue University.

The second time I quit was final. It was during my fifth year at Purdue. I was redshirted as a freshman, meaning that I attended all the practices, meetings, and strength and conditioning trainings that year, but I did not play in games, qualifying me for a fifth year of eligibility. The redshirt is used for several reasons, but one of the most common is to allow an extra year of maturity and growth for young athletes to better prepare for the physical and emotional demands of Division 1 football. I was also a good student, and this redshirt year provided the opportunity for me to get off to a strong start academically.

Once I started playing in games the following year, I did well, and over the next three years, I played well enough to have a successful career individually. I started more than twenty games between 1987 and 1989, earned Academic All-Big Ten honors three times, was named to the Academic All-America second team in 1988, and was a finalist for the prestigious Anson Mount Award, which at that time was given annually to the top scholar football player. I was also named by several publications to the 1989 preseason All-Big Ten team, which was a testament to my strong growth as a player.

But the truth is, I never really loved playing football. I played because I had the size and ability, and it was a path to achieve my educational goals without my parents or me incurring college loan debt. I did like playing in games, but I didn't love it, and I certainly didn't like all the other stuff that went along with it. It was not my passion. But it was also something others wanted me to do. They projected their dreams onto me to want to play professionally, and so I would say that I wanted to play in the National Football League and that this was my dream. But deep down, that wasn't true, even though at the time I didn't recognize it or want to admit it. I wasn't being authentic with myself.

When you don't authentically desire something, you don't assuredly believe in or have passion for it. This lack of true passion may not be evident until one day when you reach a crossroad where you have to make a decision that will test your authentic self.

I started to reach that point late in the fall of 1989. I had experienced several injuries over the prior year. I'd had two surgeries on my right knee within a six-month period, and it had become degenerative, resulting in constant pain and excessive swelling. In fact, the doctor told me that, from his analysis, my knee had aged the equivalent of thirty years in six months. He said, "Your twenty-one-year-old right knee has as much wear as I would expect in a fifty-one-year-old's. Well, at least you know what it feels like to get old."

To play in games in 1989, I had to have my knee drained of excess fluid before each kickoff. The needles they used then were more similar to the ones used today to inject turkeys with liquid seasoning. The fluid they extracted had the appearance, consistency, and viscosity of motor oil. Finally, after the sixth week of having my knee drained, the doctors said that it was no longer an option and ruled me out for the remainder of the season.

Five months later, my knee had improved enough for me to participate in spring football. I had put on about ten pounds of muscle and was very strong and relatively healthy. I was excited that I could be on the verge of a big final season. Then one day at practice during a pass rushing drill, I got injured. I had exploded off the line using a speed rush technique on the offensive tackle, dipped my left shoulder, and planted my right foot to cut a sharp angle to get around him when I felt my right big toe pop. I immediately stopped and tried to walk it off. But it quickly got worse. It was an injury called turf toe, and if you've never had it, you can't understand how painful it is. It's especially painful for a football player because everything you do is on the balls of your feet, and therefore most of your weight and force is on your big toe joint. The injury was bad enough that I was unable to participate in the remainder of spring practice. I could tell the coaches were not happy with me. From their comments, it was clear that they were thinking back to my knee injury that ended my 1989 season, and with this second injury ending my spring football season, their view was that either I wasn't tough enough, wasn't trying hard enough to get healthy, or didn't care.

Over the summer, I stayed on campus for the first time in my career and trained hard with the team, putting on another fifteen pounds of muscle. I rehabbed the turf toe consistently, and it improved slightly. It certainly was not healed, and I was not 100 percent, but I had trained hard and wanted to go out strong in my last year. When three-a-day practices (three different two-hour practices in one day for two straight weeks) began at the start of the 1990 season, I felt like I had to find a way to play through the pain and hope that maybe it would get better. Unfortunately, I reinjured it the first day of practice in full pads. This time it was much worse than before and much more painful. I sat out the next few days of practice, but I was on the field dressed in shorts as my injured status dictated, and the coaches made their feelings very clear again that they were unhappy with me.

The next day when I went to practice, again dressed in shorts, the head coach ran over and accosted me in front of my teammates. "I'm tired of this. As far as I'm concerned, you're not injured, so if you have any character at all, go put on your pads and get back here for a full practice." I almost quit right then, but I didn't want to look weak in front of my teammates. I limped back to the locker room, got dressed, and limped back to the practice field as fast as I could. The coach was waiting for me and yelled, "Hey, Leggett, you're not hurt, so stop limping and get in those drills now!"

I got in line with the rest of the defensive linemen and went through the rope drills. How I was able to make it through those drills I will never know, because I experienced the most pain that I have ever felt in my life. I knew right then that there was no way I could get through that practice. After the drill I took off my helmet, went to the sideline, and took a knee. The head coach came over and said, "You just stay there. We're going to meet after practice." I don't remember much about the rest of that practice, because I was distracted by the pain and by my anger at the coach. Ironically, I don't remember thinking that this might be the last time I would be on the field with my teammates.

I met with the head coach in his office after practice. He took a slightly less aggressive tone in the meeting than he had on the field, but he was much more condescending. I tried to explain my injury and the pain I was in, but he didn't want to hear it. He talked about how he was disappointed in my leadership, about how I had let my teammates down, and about how the team had a chance to win but needed senior leadership from players like me who will sacrifice for the team and play through pain. He said, "I want you on this team, but if you're going to be here, you have to commit to doing whatever it takes, and if you can't, then you shouldn't come back."

I once again tried to explain to him that it wasn't just that I was in tremendous pain but that I was really injured. I told him that I felt like he thought I wasn't injured at all and also that he was wrong to yell at me, especially in front of the team, and make me go through those drills to prove a point. I reminded him how I'd played through many injuries before, including a degenerative knee. It hurt me to know that he and the other coaches thought I was faking or was simply not tough enough. I told him that I sacrificed for the team and did what it took to play through injuries by playing three games with a broken finger and six games after having my knee drained just to be able to walk. He said, "Well, you need to do it again. Do whatever it takes to play if you're committed to this team. If you can do that, then I'll see you tomorrow at practice." I told him I'd be back the next day.

I went to my apartment, closed the door to my bedroom, and sat down to think. My first thought was, *What do I have to do to get well enough to play?* I considered going to the head trainer and team doctor and asking for painkillers or direct pain injections into my toe. But then I started thinking about the long-term ramifications and then asked myself what my ultimate objective was. I knew my chances of being drafted into the NFL were low due to my injury history. There was no way I would pass the predraft physical because my knee was degenerative and would only get worse. And at that point, I was in so much pain that I wasn't sure if my toe would ever improve, and even if I did take painkillers to play, it would certainly lead to another degenerative joint.

Then I asked myself, deep down, if I really wanted to play in the NFL anyway. After a few moments of intense contemplation, the answer came to me, and it was a resolute no. I had only been holding on to this so-called dream because it was always what I said I wanted and what other people expected me to want. Once I reached this realization, that I authentically and assuredly did not want to play professional football, I had the mental freedom to think seriously about giving up my last year of eligibility and ending my career.

On the one hand, I thought about how cool it would be to play my final year with all the guys I came in with and go out together. We had all gone through so much together, including the coaching staff who recruited us being fired midway through our freshman year, yet most of us persevered and stayed with the program. But on the other hand, I just wasn't willing to continue risking my body and my well-being or to keep playing for coaches who I no longer respected. The team was also coming off four straight losing seasons, and contrary to what the coach said, I did not think this team was close to winning, regardless of senior leadership. I also thought about the fact that I wasn't just an athlete but a student-athlete, and I had not given my all to my studies. I was a good student, but I wondered how much better I could be if I was able to focus all my energy on my courses. Finally, I thought about how people were questioning my character and commitment. I knew my character was strong, and I realized that I didn't have to prove anything to anyone and that I didn't owe anything to anyone, except myself.

I didn't go back.

When I didn't show up for practice the next day, the coach called the team together and announced that I had quit on them. It was painful to hear this from my teammates. But honestly, the disappointment was fleeting and couldn't diminish the freedom I felt from finally acknowledging my authentic self and doing what I wanted to do.

When people would ask me about it, for a while I refrained from saying I quit. I would instead say that I decided to not play my fifth year or that I stopped playing football in 1990. But the fact is that I did quit. Facing the reality that quitting was the right thing for me was truly freeing and allowed me to break out of the cycle of no destiny control. It prepared me for my personal transformation to later create my life plan and take full control of my destiny.

The Destiny Development Delta model will help you transform and build the capability to have the authentic self-insight, plan, assured belief, and hope needed to escape the cycle of no destiny control and transform your life. But before we move into the model overview, I want to ensure that you understand *transformation*. Because for the Destiny Development Delta model to truly work for you, you will have to commit to transform yourself.

Change is not enough; commitment to transformation will be required to make your destiny happen.

CHAPTER 5

THE IMPORTANCE OF UNDERSTANDING TRANSFORMATION VERSUS CHANGE

Change is usually defined as making something different in some way, modifying, adjusting, or turning in another direction. As the definition implies, change entails moving from one path to another or altering how things are done. In this way, those initiating the change view the necessary adaptations or adjustments as improving their chances for success or the modifications required to better meet new circumstances. In other words, the entity is the same, but a behavior or a small set of behaviors or direction is altered, or there are adjustments to strategies and tactics deployed. In essence, a change is an adjustment to circumstances or environment or a new dynamic to give you the best chance to accomplish your goals.

To illustrate the practical meaning of change, consider a sports team during a given season. The coach has a plan to win the league championship that details the style by which the team will play and the makeup of the players to ensure that they best fit that strategy. For each game, the coach makes a plan that includes adjustments to the strategy based on the other team's tendencies as observed in their previous games. During each game, the coach notes how the other team is playing and what their strategy appears to be, how the referees are calling the game, the crowd noise, the weather and other environmental variables, and how his team is playing. Then he adjusts his game plan and the player rotations to improve the team's chances of winning that game. The team is essentially the same and the overall strategy to win a championship is still in place, but changes have been made in each game to adjust to opponents and circumstances.

A simpler example of change is a chameleon. When threatened or when entering an area where it feels it stands out too much, a chameleon changes color to adjust to the new circumstance or environment. Therefore, when a chameleon moves from dirt to grass, it changes its color from brown to green. However, even though it has changed, it is still a chameleon. It has just changed its color. The key here is that change is usually something that one can come back from. *Change is not a point of no return.* You always know that if change doesn't work out, you can go back to the way it was before.

FIGURE 5.1: CHANGE CHARACTERIZED BY THE CHAMELEON

Although change requires a lot of diligence and work, sometimes it's not enough to achieve the objective you're striving for. There are times when something completely new and different is needed. Maybe you assess that a modification of the current plan is not enough, and a wholly new plan is required. Or you realize that a handful of personal changes in behaviors is not enough and a complete and dramatic makeover, both inside and out, is necessary. In these cases, what's needed is a transformation to something entirely new and different.

Transformation, as defined by the *Merriam-Webster* dictionary, is "to make radically different; the act of transforming or to transform meaning to change the composition of or structure." As the definition implies, transformation entails converting the composition of the entity itself. It is less about changing a behavior or adjusting a plan. The overall essence and composition are transformed; in other words, there is a significant alteration of the individual. It is about transforming the core of the entity or person themselves not only to meet the needs of new circumstances but also to achieve higher-order objectives possibly considered out of reach or impossible before the transformation.

Let's return to the sports team analogy to illustrate transformation. The team's owners review the overall strategy following an unsuccessful season and decide, given that the league has changed significantly, that minor modifications to strategy will not be enough to make them real competitors for the championship. They decide to take a transformative approach. They introduce a completely new strategy and replace the entire coaching staff and all the players to align to it. To make things even more radically different, they relocate the team to a new city and adopt a new name, new uniforms, and new team colors. The overall goal of winning the championship is still in place, but the strategy and the team have been transformed.

A simpler example is a caterpillar. A caterpillar lives part of its life in one specific form. However, at some point the caterpillar must make the decision to transform itself. It creates a cocoon. When it eventually emerges, it has now transformed into a butterfly. Unlike the chameleon that changes its color but still remains a chameleon, the caterpillar has taken on a completely different form and is no longer a caterpillar. Its old form is no more. The key here is that transformation is something you can't come back from. *Transformation is a point of no return.* The butterfly cannot turn back into a caterpillar. That way of life is over, and the behaviors that went along with it are gone. With transformation, the reality is that you cannot go back to the way it was before.

FIGURE 5.2: TRANSFORMATION CHARACTERIZED BY THE BUTTERFLY

It should be clear at this point that there is a monumental difference between change and transformation. Change is about altering direction while transformation is about altering who you are. Change is about modifying your behaviors while transformation is about modifying yourself. Change can be temporary, and you have to work every day to make change sustainable by fighting against external and internal factors trying to push back to the norm of the prior behavior. Transformation is permanent because the core composition and structure have been converted to a new amalgamation.

We have all heard it before: Change is hard. We build habits, and those habits become patterns of behaviors that then become ingrained. Breaking away from these ingrained behaviors can be very difficult. So yes, change is hard, but transformation is even harder. Transformation is much harder to envision and to do because it challenges us at the core. However, it can also be viewed as easier, in a way, because once a transformation has taken hold, it is permanent and thus sustains by definition. It's not about changing behaviors but about transforming who you are from the core, from the inside out, and then the behaviors will follow.

The key ingredient driving transformation is your authentic reason to transform. For a personal transformation, the reason must be intrinsic (from inside yourself) to be authentic. If it is extrinsic (from outside yourself or from someone else), it will be a glorified change masquerading as a transformation. This is because the compelling reason did not originate from inside the person, from their authentic self-insight. It is not from the heart. It may feel deeply heartfelt, because the person might be doing it to make someone important to them happy, but it is not what their heart truly wants for themselves. Thus, deep down, subconsciously the person can't fully commit to the transformation. They may be able to fool others and even themselves by faking it and portraying success and happiness, but because they never authentically transformed, they are more than likely suffering deep inside. This is not sustainable.

Conversely, if your reason is authentically intrinsic and truly emanates from self-insight, passion, and heart, it exponentially improves your odds of successful transformation. This is because you are inspiring yourself by being in touch with your own heart and mind. It is undeniable that the most compellingly authentic and assured inspiration to transform comes from your self-sight and your heart. If your heart is compelled to transform, and deep down you know this is what you want, there is no such thing as apathetic compliance; there is only passionate commitment.

Developing your authentic, assured, and intrinsic inspiration to transform that so clearly defines your true life goal, that you feel you can overcome any fear and obstacle, takes time, tremendous energy, and self-insight. But when done correctly, it is the single best predictor of a successful transformation. It has been said many times that an average strategy with great buy-in will always beat great strategy with average buy-in, and this applies not only to groups but also to individuals. This is exactly what one of my mentors told me when the organization I took over just months prior completely turned around from historically poor performance. When I asked him why things were advancing so quickly when I hadn't even implemented the improvement plan yet, he said, "Never underestimate the power of people just liking you. You are inspiring them with your belief in them." It always begins with authentically touching hearts, starting with yours, to inspire transformation.

If you are centered and have an authentic heart-first approach, you can help drive a transformation in others. This is important because sometimes you can feel that as one person, you are insignificant and can't make a difference. But we forget the power of exponential influence. It's like the butterfly effect, which is the theory that when a butterfly flaps its wings in a garden, it could help create a hurricane or tornado hundreds of miles away. It's hard to believe that something so small can have a such monumental effect until you think about it this way: What if the conditions were right and that one butterfly flapped its wings in the same direction at the same exact time as all the other millions of butterflies? That one flap could be the last wind force needed to pass the tipping point to create the hurricane.

This is similar to the exponential effect that individuals can have through interpersonal influence. If I am able to influence two people to volunteer for a good cause, and they influence two people each, and those four influence two people each, and those eight influence two people each, my individual impact has been magnified thirty times the original of just me alone. Now imagine that if you influenced ten people in your network of friends and family, and they influenced ten people in their networks, and those one hundred influenced ten each in their networks, and those one thousand influenced ten more each in their networks. Your individual impact would now be magnified over 11,000 times the original of just you alone.

Any one person can influence others to make a tremendous impact. You are not insignificant, unless you hold yourself back. By leveraging the Destiny Development Delta model to transform yourself, you develop the confidence and mindful clarity not only to take control of your life and destiny but also to influence others and drive positive societal change much larger than yourself. With all the massive challenges facing our world today, there has never been a greater need for positive influence leaders than right now. You can make your destiny happen and make a difference in society.

I have many examples of personally influencing transformation in others that I could share, but the best of these is the story of a man I will refer to as Bill.

I worked with Bill early in my professional career at a large US manufacturing plant in the mid-West. I had recently graduated from university and was hired as an engineer in the plant, but at the time, I was training as a night shift supervisor. Bill had thirty years at the plant and was the lead operator on one of the largest systems, but he also had a reputation of being an unpleasant person. Most people simply avoided him.

The first time I met Bill, I visited the control room to check in on him. I said hello and asked if he needed anything, but he refused to look up or respond, then stormed out. This went on for the first two weeks I was on night shift. During the third week, I decided to structure my shift rounds to allow more time in Bill's control room to see if I could establish some semblance of a relationship with him. Now when he stormed out, I would follow him and ask if he could teach me some of the key technical aspects of his production system. He responded only with grunts, but he would at least point to key dials and gauges, and he handed me the operator control manual to read. When I went home, I studied the manual, and when I saw Bill in his control room the next night, I asked him some questions about the line that were not in the book, which made it obvious that I had read it. Bill still would not speak, but if I asked a yes or no question, he would nod or shake his head, and if the question needed more explanation, he would get up and motion for me to follow him, then point out things on the line that led me to the answer.

The fourth week, I felt there had been enough of a breakthrough to enable a dialogue between us. Up to this point, Bill had not said one word to me, only grunts. This time when I visited Bill's control room, I shared some personal information, such as where I was from, my family in Key West, living in the mid-West, even playing college football in the Big Ten, which almost all the older guys in the plant were interested in hearing about. Bill listened and didn't storm out, but he never responded until I talked about how I liked to fish in Key West and that I loved eating saltwater fish but that I'd never been freshwater fishing or knew much about it. Bill turned and looked at me, which was a shock in and of itself, but then he spoke! He said how he loved to fish in fresh water. How peaceful it was and how it allowed him to clear his head. He talked about how delicious freshwater fish is and that, in his opinion, it's better than saltwater fish. He said that he could meet me in the middle with salmon, which is found in both fresh and salt water. (Salmon are anadromous, which means that they are born and reproduce in fresh water but live most of their lives in salt water.) He asked if I ever had deep-fried salmon, and I replied that I didn't think people deep-fried salmon. Bill told me that he would bring me some the next night to try.

That next night Bill came into the plant early so that he could stop by the supervisor's office to give me the fish. I will never forget the moment Bill entered the office to talk to me. All the older supervisors stopped and looked at him like *Oh no. What is he up to?* When he approached my desk, I saw that several supervisors had incredulous looks on their faces. Bill took out the fish and explained that he'd brought two types, fried salmon and fried walleye, a very popular freshwater fish. He'd also brought a photo album and showed me pictures of his family.

When Bill left the office, one of the older supervisors named Jim, who had been at the plant for about forty years, said, "Don't eat that fish." I asked him why not. He said, "Didn't you see the way we all looked at that guy when he came in?" I said that I had and asked why. He responded, "First, he's just overall not a good guy, to anyone. He's a jerk and a blowhard. But I have to tell you that he's also a card-carrying member of the Ku Klux Klan! So if I were you, I would not eat that fish."

I was shocked, to say the least, but it felt to me that Bill was sincere. I told Jim that clearly Bill was not a good guy before, and he still may not be, but I felt like somehow I had connected with him and that he was changing. I took a big chance and ate the fish, because I knew that Bill would ask me during the shift what I thought, and I wanted to continue to be authentic with him. The fish was great, and the relationship that Bill and I developed continued to grow. I was basically the only person in the plant who Bill talked to and had a relationship with. He became one of my biggest supporters while I worked there, consistently going out of his way to help ensure my success.

However, the story doesn't end there. Little did I know that the change that I helped spark in Bill eventually led to a dramatic and unbelievable transformation. A couple of years after I left the company, I received a letter from Bill. When I opened it, I was absolutely amazed by what I saw. It was an engagement announcement. On the back were the preprinted details of the engagement along with a handwritten note from Bill to me. In the note Bill wrote, "I wanted you to know the full impact that you had on my life. When I met you, I was going through a divorce, and it was a tough time for me. You were the only one who took the time to talk to me, and your persistence to get to know me, no matter how big the barriers I put up, showed me that someone still saw me as a person worth knowing. I know that you knew about my past racist beliefs and affiliations, but you stuck with me. I have completely transformed into someone else, someone better because you treated me like a person. I am happy now, as happy as I have ever been. Thanks so much for helping me see the light and let my true self come out, and please never change." On the other side of the engagement announcement was a picture of Bill and his fiancée, who just happened to be a Black woman. I had sparked Bill's transformation from an unhappy, hateful racist to a happy, loving anti-racist. If you ever think that you, as one person, are insignificant and can't have an impact, think about me and Bill.

Everyone has the power to inspire and drive change and transformation. As I will discuss in more detail later in this book, to inspire means having the ability to influence, move, or guide by divine or supernatural inspiration. This was brought to life in the story of Bill's incredible transformation, because it is about influencing people to transform themselves in ways they never thought possible. His is one of the most important stories presented in this book because it clearly and vividly illustrates the power of one person's ability to inspire and the incredible magnitude of transformation that can be achieved.

As I stated in the beginning, I feel that everyone should believe that they can develop the capability to control their destiny. Without this belief, there will be an increasing lack of hope in our collective futures. Reestablishing hope is important, but without a plan, it will erode itself and slip into despair and hopelessness. But it doesn't have to be that way if you have authentic hope. This is hope that comes from true self-insight, assured belief, and genuine intrinsic drive, coupled with an authentic plan. The combination of authentic hope and an authentic plan is powerful and will energize and fuel your transformation, allowing you to escape from the cycle of no destiny control. This is why I am committed to inspiring and coaching you through the Destiny Development Delta model for transformational success—to provide you with the tools and capability to make your destiny happen.

SECTION 3
DESTINY DEVELOPMENT DELTA MODEL OVERVIEW

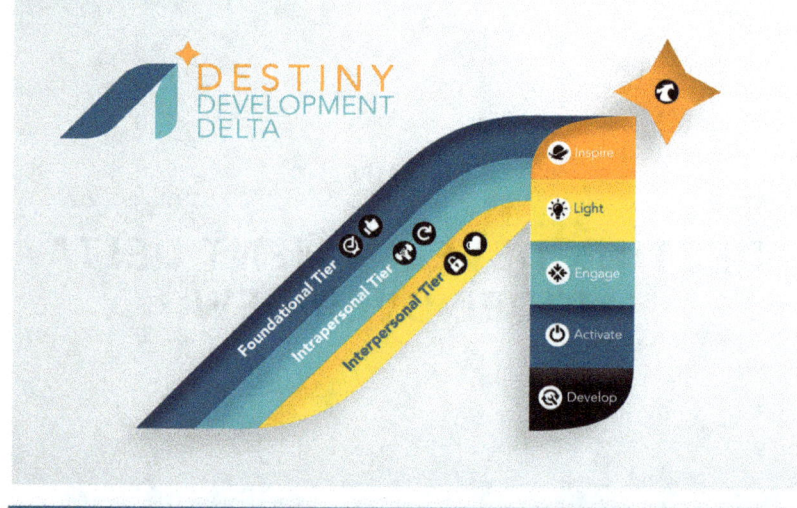

CHAPTER 6

MAIN MESSAGES OF SECTION 3

The purpose of this section is to provide an overview of the Destiny Development Delta model, illustrate what it is designed to do, and introduce the overall deployment process. In section 3, I will cover the following key summary points:

- The Destiny Development Delta model begins and ends with personal transformation.
- The model continually evolves to keep you on track with your long-term life goals. *Destiny* refers to the future state of your life, *development* refers to continuous learning and adaptation, and *delta* represents ongoing dynamic change.
- The model was created to drive a personal transformation by integrating the *how* of the personal transformation, called the A-attitudes of leadership model, and the *what* of the personal transformation, called the iLEAD change model. This integration is what differentiates the Destiny Development Delta model from all others.
- The A-attitudes of leadership model initiates and sustains personal transformation and is divided into four tiers: the foundational tier of authenticity and assuredness, the intrapersonal tier of accountability and action, the interpersonal tier of accessibility and adoration, and the apex tier of amalgamation.

- The iLEAD change model provides a clearly defined road map to operationalize personal transformation by building and activating the life plan to take control of one's destiny. The model is comprised of five elements: inspiration, light, engage, activate, and develop.
- The process for deploying the Destiny Development Delta model encompasses three major milestones that are introduced in section 3 and that are the subject of sections 4 through 6.

CHAPTER 7

DESTINY DEVELOPMENT DELTA MODEL INTRODUCTION

It's not hard to understand that with all the complexity, distraction, and uncertainty described in section 2, many people feel that they are not in control of their own lives and destiny. But as also explained in section 2, it doesn't have to be this way. You can control your destiny by transforming yourself and creating the inner strength and resiliency needed to consistently strive to be the best you can be while maintaining your well-being. You can escape the cycle of no destiny control. You're probably thinking, *That's easy to say, but how do I do it? Where do I start? How do I know what the right approach is? There's so much advice and so many programs out there, it's hard to tell which is best for me.*

You're correct that there's an ever-growing multitude of opinions, programs, TED Talks, podcasts, and books on the key to success. For some it's the ability to be creative while others say it's self-confidence; still others say it's strategic thinking, courage to act, hard work, networking, acting with boldness, having a growth mindset, or being a disrupter. With all these buzzword choices, it can be overwhelming and confusing to know which is best. And although all are said to be the key to success, none are a perfect fit for all people because they weren't designed to be ubiquitously applied. Most originated from studies of highly successful subgroups, almost always business leaders. Their so-called success factors were then distilled down to one or two key points that became the slogan program. Other critical variables were ignored, deemed insignificant, or assumed to be present with everyone and thus not difference makers, resulting in proclamations that if you follow our program, you can be the next Jeff Bezos.

This clearly is not realistic. One of these programs may apply to some people, where all the variables line up or the circumstances come together, but it will not work for most people, because most people have unique circumstances and variables that do not align with the very specific and narrow nature of these programs. Unfortunately, this leads many to choose a program recommended to them by someone who thinks it might apply to them, and if it doesn't feel right or yield the outcomes expected, they switch to another program, then another, or eventually give up.

The Destiny Development Delta model, on the other hand, is designed to facilitate your specific personal transformation by integrating our proprietary models, the A-attitudes of leadership and the iLEAD change concepts, to build the unique capability and individualized road map that you need to take control of your life and make your destiny happen.

Other programs or models mostly espouse behavioral change to again mimic some successful businessperson or personality. Others may tell you to transform, but they don't provide the *how* to practically do this in a sustained way or the *what* to leverage your transformation into long-term success and legacy. The Destiny Development Delta model helps you personally transform from within, then turns your transformation into the real action of identifying your desired destiny, putting it into a plan, and bringing it to life. No other program does that. This is what differentiates the Destiny Development Delta model from all others.

To understand the Destiny Development Delta model, we must first begin with the meanings of the words and how they work together. Destiny is defined by *Merriam-Webster* as "something to which a person or thing is destined; a predetermined course of events often held to be an irresistible power or agency." Generally, it is thought of as predetermined future fate. In the case of our model, we define destiny as the future state of your life and legacy that you decide. It's not a fate in which you have no say; it's within your agency or control and determined by the actions you take every moment of every day. And because it's based on both planned and unplanned actions and reactions to external stimuli, it is by definition dynamic.

Development is defined by *Merriam-Webster* as "the act, process, or result of developing, or state of being developed." It's generally thought of as levels of growth or advancement. The word *development* specific to our model is the ongoing learning, capability building, and adaptability we must have to grow and adjust to the dynamic changes our environment, times, and society generates. It is absolutely a requirement to both adjust to changes in the environment and stay on track and/or ahead of the capability needed to achieve the destiny life plan. Education and continuous learning are critical to development, like the Nobel Prize winner and legendary former president of South Africa, Nelson Mandela, said: "Education is the most powerful weapon which you can use to change the world." Additionally, the word *develop* also includes the continuous improvement of important capabilities that we have learned or attained, as Brazilian national treasure and renowned soccer player of the twentieth century, Pelé, made clear in only three words: "Everything is practice." But ultimately, development as part of the Destiny Development Delta model is all about the lifelong pursuit to continually make yourself better, as twenty-three-time Grand Slam title winner Serena Williams said: "I think in life you should work on yourself until the day you die."

Delta is defined by *Merriam-Webster* as "something shaped like a capital Greek delta, or in *mathematics*, an increment of a variable." But it is also generally used in math and physics to represent change or transformation in the formula or an aspect of the formula. The word *delta* specific to our model is the never-ending dynamic change that we face in our lives and in the world every day that we must recognize and respect, make adjustments to our destiny plan when appropriate, and continuously develop ourselves to successfully grow. But most importantly, delta in this model represents transformation—the personal transformation that must take place to ensure the long-term success of your life plan goal. Drake, the Canadian music artist who has sold more than two hundred million records and who is the most streamed artist of all time, said, "Life can always change; you have to adjust."

The entire model works together in a harmonic symphony of well-orchestrated jazz to successfully navigate the complexity and dynamic challenges of life in our world and in society. And just like jazz, the model is structured yet alive and adaptable (to small, large, short-term, and long-term challenges that will arise) and does not have a shelf life. This is one of the most unique and differentiating aspects of the model.

CHAPTER 8

DESTINY DEVELOPMENT DELTA INTEGRATED MODEL OVERVIEW

The Destiny Development Delta model drives personal transformation by integrating the A-attitudes of leadership and the iLEAD change concepts into a truly holistic model that, if followed, will build your capability to take control of your life and make your destiny happen. The model drives transformation from the inside out by developing holistic balance and personal well-being and operationalizes it by building the life plan and providing the tools, processes, and models to activate and sustain it.

FIGURE 8.1: THE DESTINY DEVELOPMENT DELTA MODEL

The Destiny Development Delta model is comprised of the *how* of the individual's transformation into one capable of striving to be the best and controlling one's destiny. This is the foundation and backbone of the model and is called the A-attitudes of leadership, which are a set of personal leadership values that together help develop your holistic balance and personal well-being. They are divided into four tiers: the foundational tier (authenticity and assuredness), the intrapersonal tier (accountability and action), the interpersonal tier (accessibility and adoration), and the apex tier (amalgamation). I will cover the A-attitudes of leadership in detail in section 4.

FIGURE 8.2: THE A-ATTITUDES OF LEADERSHIP MODEL

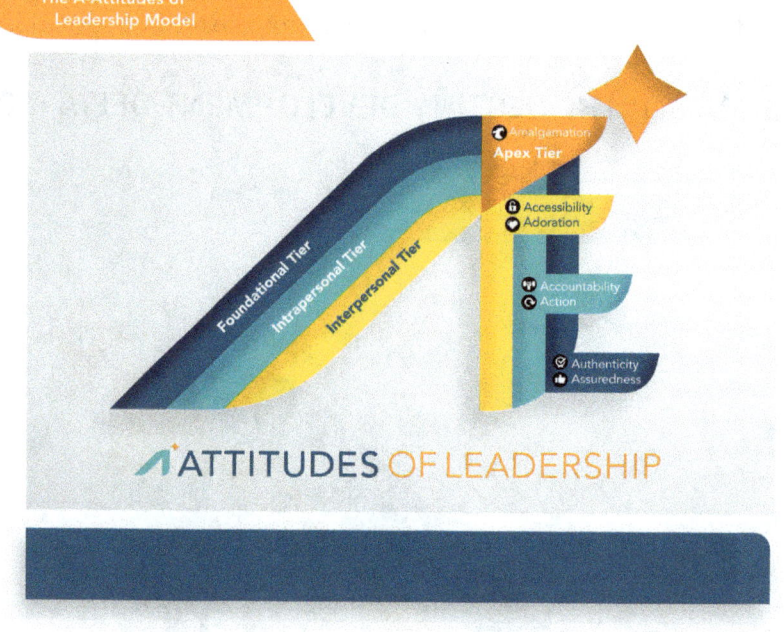

The Destiny Development Delta model is also comprised of the *what*, which is an iterative and clearly defined road map for the individual to operationalize their transformation by building their life plan, or personal action plan, and by developing all the support structures and systems to sustainably activate the plan, for them to actually take control and achieve the success and happiness they desire for their destiny. This road map provides that path forward as part of the Destiny Development Delta model and is called iLEAD change, which is a descriptive acronym made up of the five directive words: inspire, light, engage, activate, and develop. I will cover iLEAD change in detail in section 5.

FIGURE 8.3: THE iLEAD CHANGE MODEL

The integration of the A-attitudes of leadership model, which drives the internal holistic transformation with holistic balance and personal well-being, with the iLEAD change model, which drives the external operationalization of the model by building and activating the life plan, together create the ability to take control of your life and destiny. This is the essence of the Destiny Development Delta integrated model.

FIGURE 8.4: THE DESTINY DEVELOPMENT DELTA INTEGRATED MODEL

CHAPTER 9

THE THREE MAJOR MILESTONES OF THE DESTINY DEVELOPMENT DELTA MODEL DEPLOYMENT PROCESS

The Destiny Development Delta model drives personal transformation by integrating the A-attitudes of leadership and the iLEAD change concepts into a truly holistic model that, if followed, will guarantee your success. This is what differentiates our model.

The deployment process for the Destiny Development Delta model includes the following three major milestones:

1. The A-attitudes of leadership model
2. The iLEAD change model
3. The formula for success

FIGURE 9.1: THE THREE MAJOR MILESTONES

The focus of these milestones is to provide a disciplined approach to ensure the most optimum integration of the A-attitudes of leadership personal transformation for holistic balance and personal well-being, the creation of the life plan and iLEAD change capability building, and the coaching support processes to sustainably activate the plan over time. This represents a rigorous process that requires personal commitment and work, but if successfully completed, it will guarantee that you will take control of your life and destiny.

What follows is an overview of the contents and deliverables for each of the milestones for the deployment process, followed by sections 4 through 6, which are dedicated to each of the milestones and will present detailed explanations as well as associated models, processes, and tools that are specifically designed to assist in the completion of each milestone.

MILESTONE 1: THE A-ATTITUDES OF LEADERSHIP MODEL

The objective of this milestone is to build A-attitudes of leadership capability to develop the self-awareness, holistic balance, and personal well-being required to initiate and sustain your transformation to control your destiny. The foundational tier of authenticity and assuredness enables you to leverage the intrapersonal tier of action and accountability, the interpersonal tier of accessibility and adoration, and the apex tier of amalgamation to couple with iLEAD change to begin building and activating your life plan.

MILESTONE 2: THE iLEAD CHANGE MODEL

The objective of the second milestone is to build iLEAD change capability to create and activate your life plan, including understanding the tools, models, and processes to fully and continually activate it over time. It begins with the *inspire* section, which is focused on leveraging the A-attitudes of leadership developed in milestone 1 to build a life plan that is true to yourself. The next section, *light*, is focused on creating the clarity of communication of your life plan to successfully inspire yourself and others and recruit their support. *Engage* is the next section, which is building your capability to develop networks and relationships and to leverage your clarity of plan and communications to recruit supporters. The penultimate section is *activate*, which is all about bringing your plan to life and making it happen over time to achieve your life goals. The final section is *develop*, which is continuously learning and building new capabilities to enable you to quickly adjust and adapt to stay on track as both planned and unplanned life, environmental, and social changes inevitably come your way.

MILESTONE 3: THE FORMULA FOR SUCCESS

The objective of this final milestone is to leverage the formula for success to launch and, most importantly, sustain the journey to take control of your destiny. The Destiny Development Delta formula for success is a proprietary process to ensure that your adoption of our model results in successful personal transformation and development and activation of your life plan and sets you firmly on track to sustainably control your destiny. The formula for success is comprised of three principal aspects:

1. *The comprehensive Destiny Development Delta model deployment process:* Completing the comprehensive deployment process is the first step in the formula for success.
2. *Progress tracking and measurement assessment:* The second aspect is the proprietary assessment processes to gauge progress and identify gaps and areas of opportunity to fortify learning and ensure readiness to progress through the model deployment milestones.
3. *Dedicated coaching, mentoring, and support:* The third aspect is dedicated coaching, mentoring, and support to facilitate the personal transformation and construction of the life plan, translate the progress tracking into learning and capability adjustments as needed, and guide and coach the critically important year-one launch and activation of the life plan.

In summary, our three-milestone deployment process, comprised of the A-attitudes of leadership, iLEAD change and the formula for success, will guarantee your transformation as well as the construction and activation of your legacy path. This is again what differentiates the Destiny Development Delta model from all others.

SECTION 4

MILESTONE 1: THE A-ATTITUDES OF LEADERSHIP MODEL

Destiny Development Delta Model
The Three Major Milestones of the Deployment Model and Key Deliverables

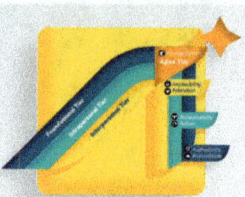  

ATTITUDES
OF LEADERSHIP

The A-Attitudes of Leadership Personal Transformation Model

Holistic Balance and Personal Well-being

The A-Attitudes of Leadership Capability, Development to Support Your Transformation

iLEAD
CHANGE

Destiny Development Delta Life Plan

iLEAD Change Capability, Processes, and Models to Activate Your Life Plan

FORMULA
FOR SUCCESS

The Comprehensive Destiny Development Delta Model Deployment Process

Progress Tracking and Measurement Assessment

Dedicated Coaching, Mentoring, and Support

CHAPTER 10

MAIN MESSAGES OF SECTION 4

In this section, I will describe and explain the following:
- The A-attitudes of leadership model and its importance in powering your personal transformation to take control of your life and make your destiny happen.
- The foundational tier of authenticity (deeply knowing and being true to yourself) and assuredness (believing and being confident in yourself) and why this tier underscores the critical importance of foundation building on which to support your transformation.
- The intrapersonal tier of accountability (keeping your commitments) and action (actually doing) and why this tier is important in terms of your ability to personally and credibly deliver and live up to your authentic and assured self.
- The interpersonal tier of accessibility (availability to others) and adoration (love of others) and why this tier is important in terms of your ability to fully relate to and build relationships with others.
- The apex tier of amalgamation (everything coming together to complete your transformation), why this tier is important, and how it ensures that you are ready for milestone 2 (the iLEAD change model).
- Holistic balance and personal well-being development.
- The A-attitudes of leadership personal transformation self-assessment, which is designed to cement your transformational learning and understanding of the A-attitudes of leadership model.

CHAPTER 11

THE A-ATTITUDES OF LEADERSHIP MODEL

In this section, I will explain the A-attitudes of leadership model in greater depth and provide several personal stories and examples to vividly bring each A-attitude of leadership capability to life while also introducing a few proprietary coaching and development models and processes.

FIGURE 11.1: DESTINY DEVELOPMENT DELTA MODEL MILESTONE 1: THE A-ATTITUDES OF LEADERSHIP

The A-attitudes of leadership model is the commencement of the Destiny Development Delta model because it builds the self-awareness, holistic balance, and personal well-being needed to initiate and sustain your transformation. Only you know who you really are, what you really want, and how badly you want it. And only you can motivate yourself every day to make it happen. The A-attitudes of leadership are quite simply the secret sauce of your personal transformation because they build the authentic self-insight and internal drive you need to passionately pursue your goal of controlling your destiny.

Remember that the A-attitudes of leadership are a set of personal transformation behaviors that are like the foundation, walls, and floors of the Destiny Development Delta model "house" on which the transformation will be built and supported. The A-attitudes of leadership are comprised of the foundational tier of authenticity and assuredness, the intrapersonal tier of accountability and action, the interpersonal tier of accessibility and adoration, and the apex tier of amalgamation. The foundational tier bolsters your depth of self-understanding, self-insight, and self-awareness, enabling you to leverage the intrapersonal tier to activate your plan and make adjustments, then inspire and engage others through the interpersonal tier. This leads to the apex tier convergence with the iLEAD change model to begin building and activating your life plan.

The following chapters will provide detailed descriptions and examples of each of the four tiers of the A-attitudes of leadership model.

CHAPTER 12

THE A-ATTITUDES OF LEADERSHIP FOUNDATIONAL TIER

The foundational tier of the A-attitudes of leadership model is the base on which the "house" of personal transformation is built. Without authenticity and assuredness, the Destiny Development Delta model cannot stand, because they ensure that you know, accept, and believe in yourself and in your ability to persevere against all trials and tribulations as you begin your transformation. Developing a strong foundational tier allows you to flourish and become an example of the adage "what doesn't kill me makes me stronger."

Figure 12.1 highlights the foundational tier of the A-attitudes of leadership model, followed by a detailed description of the key components of the tier, authenticity and assuredness, and finally personal stories to bring the foundational tier to life.

FIGURE 12.1: THE A-ATTITUDES OF LEADERSHIP FOUNDATIONAL TIER

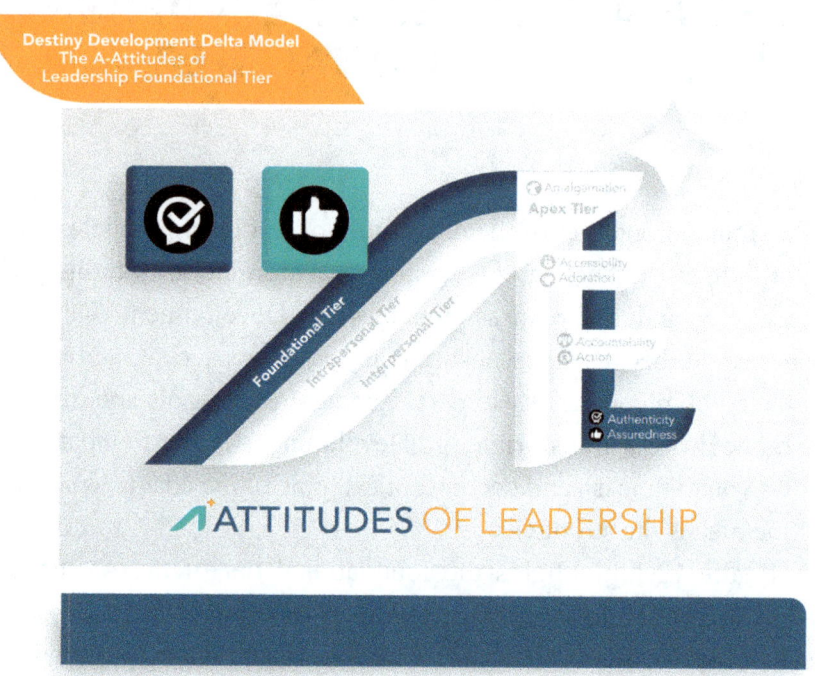

Authenticity

Authenticity establishes the foundation of the Destiny Development Delta model because you must deeply know and accept yourself before you can genuinely determine what you really want and then transform to take charge of your life. Authenticity means being real and true to one's personality, spirit, and character. It means not pretending to be someone you are not, even with yourself. It's about being proud of who you authentically are. When Viola Davis, one of the greatest actresses of our time, made her acceptance speech at the 2012 Crystal Award for Excellence in Film, she said this about authenticity: "I believe that the privilege of a lifetime is being who you are, truly being who you are. And I've spent far too long apologizing for that—my age, my color, my lack of classical beauty—that now at the age of, well, at the age of 46, I'm very proud to be Viola Davis, for whatever it's worth."

Authenticity also means getting in touch with the true you deep inside and loving that person. I am a big fan of Serena Williams. She is not only a great athlete but also an inspiration to a lot of people, based on all the things she has had to overcome in her life and career. She grew up on the public stage and has been in the spotlight for the majority of her life. Yet she has remained authentic. Here is a quote from Serena regarding loving yourself, exactly as you are: "It's me, and I love me. I learned to love me. I've been like this my whole life, and I embrace me. I love how I look. I love that I'm a full woman and I'm strong and I'm powerful and I'm beautiful at the same time. There's nothing wrong with that." This is what authenticity looks and feels like.

Assuredness

Assuredness is akin to the load-bearing walls of the A-attitudes of leadership house and is connected to and supported by the authenticity foundation. Authenticity drives self-awareness and self-acceptance, but assuredness drives self-belief. Knowing yourself allows you to stand, but believing in yourself allows you to stay upright, especially when stormy winds blow in your face.

Assuredness is defined as being characterized by certainty or security. Self-assuredness means being certain and secure in yourself personified through your authentic and assured presence. Sachin Tendulkar, the top run scorer in international cricket history and a national hero in India, said, "Presence is very important in international sport. It is one thing just being there in the middle, but it is another making people aware of your 'presence.' It is about body language and radiating confidence, something that the West Indian batting legend Viv Richards would personify."

Self-assuredness also means maintaining self-confidence even in the face of struggles. Recall the legendary statement made by Nelson Mandela, who spent twenty-seven years of his life in prison for standing against apartheid before becoming South Africa's first Black president:

"Do not judge me by my successes; judge me by how many times I fell down and got back up again."

Assuredness must be built on the foundation of authenticity because certainty can only start with deeply knowing oneself. The importance of knowing oneself is not a new concept. It has been around for thousands of years. The origination of "know thyself" has been falsely attributed to Socrates, Plato, and Aristotle in the form of "Knowing yourself is the beginning of all wisdom," but it actually originated long before, in ancient Egypt, as it appeared in hieroglyphs inscribed on various temples with the phrase "Man, know thyself and thou shalt know the gods." However, no matter how many thousands of years the wisdom of know thyself has been apparent, it is still difficult and uncomfortable for many people today who may not want to confront certain parts of themselves.

It is clear that it is uncommon to truly know and be assured in oneself, but they are key for many successful people.

- A 2010 study by Green Peak Partners and Cornell University School of Industrial and Labor Relations concluded that high self-awareness often correlates with achieving high degrees of success as a leader.
- Additional research at Cornell University showed that a high emotional self-awareness score was the strongest predictor of overall success.

Assuredness provides the wherewithal to stand up against fear and to hold yourself accountable to take action. It provides you with the ability to move forward when you are afraid or are facing the unknown. Taylor Swift, the music superstar who has repeatedly appeared on *Time* magazine's list of the 100 most influential people in the world, said, "Being fearless isn't being 100 percent not fearful; it's being terrified but you jump anyway."

Assuredness also includes being resilient, because there will be times when your self-assuredness will be tested. Again, deeply knowing one's authentic self provides the foundation from which to withstand the tumult.

Some of the most successful people in the world have demonstrated strong resiliency when their self-assuredness was challenged. J. K. Rowling was famously rejected by more than ten publishers before finding success with the Harry Potter book series. Jay-Z was rejected and ignored by big record labels before finally making it and becoming a billionaire entertainment magnate. Walt Disney was once told he wasn't creative enough before becoming one of the names most associated with creativity and having the vision and courage to build the Magic Kingdom in the middle of a swamp. Sam Walton had several store failures and filed bankruptcy before creating the Walmart empire. Michael Jordan was astonishingly cut from his high school basketball team before becoming the greatest basketball player of all time. Oprah Winfrey was told she was not fit for television before becoming a household name and arguably the most successful woman in entertainment history. Steve Jobs was fired from the company he founded before coming back years later to create the iPhone and change our world forever.

Jack Ma, the billionaire business magnate, philanthropist, and cofounder of Alibaba, was not viewed as a future visionary star of the global business world early in his life. In fact, according to Ma, "Nobody wanted to believe in Jack Ma." He had to persevere through disappointments and struggles by leveraging his self-assuredness to perpetuate his belief in himself. Ma said, "I flunked my exam for university two times before I was accepted by what was considered my city's worst university, Hangzhou Teachers University. I was studying to be a high school English teacher [but] in my university, I was elected student chairman and later became chairman of the city's Students Federation." He went on to eventually build one of the largest and most innovative e-commerce companies in the world—Alibaba.

Being authentic and self-assured go hand in hand. If you know yourself and love yourself, you will believe in yourself no matter what anyone says or thinks. I really like this quote from Serena Williams regarding not caring about what others think of you: "Think of all the girls who could become top athletes but quit sports because they're afraid of having too many defined muscles and being made fun of or called unattractive." And this is Serena on accomplishing what you want for yourself, regardless of what others say: "You just have to prove to yourself that you can go out there and be the best that you can be and not prove anything to anyone."

Of course, Serena has not let what others say or think stop her. She has managed her career her way to become not only one of the best athletes the world has ever seen but also the host of the 2024 ESPY Awards and coproducer of *In the Arena: Serena Williams*.

Here are the perspectives of two of my mentees, Steve and Shelley, regarding the foundational tier.

Steve explained it this way:

> I have always tried to follow Donzel's example of passionate inspiration of people. I have personally learned from his leadership, which will always remain with me. Specifically, the modeling of how to inspire myself and others with the passion that anything is possible. And the investment in the way he builds personal connections with everyone, including those at the very bottom. The way he empathizes with people is something that I will always try to follow and apply in my life. But this all starts with authenticity. Through the coaching and observation of Donzel as a role model, I developed the confidence to be more authentic with my teams. This was hard for me, as my team was spread over several geographies, countries, culture, and languages. I was hesitant to be open, but Donzel's coaching and modeling helped build my self-assuredness. The more of myself I shared with and gave to my team, the more our team jelled. Communications became much better, more effective and efficient. We were able to identify potential issues earlier and proactively address them, and we collaborated better than we ever did. This resulted in our best performance since I have been there and, in fact, under the toughest circumstances. Additionally, team member morale is the highest

it's been and so is mine. Because of my learning and application of authenticity and assuredness, I have been able to grow as a person and as a leader and to build the confidence to expand my leadership influence to help the team win while advancing my career and feeling fulfilled that I am doing it in the right way.

Shelley shared this:

> Through this coaching, I have significantly improved my ability to allow my authentic self to come through and to be self-assured. I have developed so much more confidence in myself. With Donzel's help, I was able to do something I hadn't done before in a detailed way over my forty-three-year life, and that is really think about what I want for myself out of life. Where do I want to be in twenty years? What do I want my legacy to be? What is most important to me? Donzel coached me to answer these questions and to develop for the first time in my life a plan that reflected me. With this plan I had the confidence and self-assuredness to start to ask clearly for what I wanted in my career. I started to get engaged in social justice issues that were authentically important to me but that I was not confident enough to do before. I prioritized my overall well-being and personal balance. My overall outlook changed and so did my spiritual, mental, and physical health. I am so much better than I was just a year ago, and I am just getting started.

The following are some personal stories to bring the A-attitudes of leadership foundational tier of authenticity and assuredness to life.

Be True to Yourself

Authenticity also means being true to yourself. I grew up in the 1970s and 1980s in the post–civil rights era, and although great progress had been made in the United States regarding equal access for all, there still were some aspects of American society that were exclusionary. To me, one of the most obvious holdovers of our country's racist history was the game of golf. Before Tiger Woods, there were virtually no PGA players of color. Additionally, the most historic golf clubs in the country, like Augusta National where the Masters tournament is played, were virtually off-limits to African Americans, with the exception of caddies, servers, cooks, janitors, and groundskeepers.

My father was a caddie during his youth at the Key West Golf Club. Although he worked there and by all accounts was a good caddie, he was forbidden to play on the course. Thus, in his eighty-eight years of living on the island, he never played the course. From my standpoint, if golf was going to be exclusionary to my father and to others like him, then I would boycott it and never play or visit a golf club.

Fast-forward to the date when I was up for my first big promotion, the opportunity to become a director at one of the largest companies in the world at twenty-nine years of age. I was self-assured that I had the capability and leadership qualities not only to be a director but also to be one of the very best at the company. I just needed the opportunity to prove it, and this was it. The promotion also represented an important milestone in my life plan career goal of becoming a C-suite executive, because as a director, I would be able to demonstrate on a larger scale to the company's top executives that I had the potential to be an officer. However, I had one reservation, and believe it or not, that was being forced to play golf.

The extended leadership team, which included the directors, met off-site as a group four times per year. At that time, these meetings always included golf as the mandatory entertainment, networking, and career-building activity. In fact, I had been told by several peers and superiors that playing golf was a critical expectation of being a director and gaining visibility for a promotion to vice president, because it was viewed as the primary way to build credibility with leadership and coalitions with peers. But many of them also shared their reservations about this expectation. This overemphasis on golf seemed to have nothing to do with focusing on business strategy and performance, which was the intent of these meetings in the first place. Certainly, the value of one's handicap is not a reliable indicator of the quality of one's leadership. And, of course, this practice was not supportive of an inclusive culture welcoming of diversity, because many on the team hated golf but felt forced to play regardless of their feelings.

Considering my history and what I was hearing from my peers, I had to decide whether to accept the promotion and continue my career with the company or to be authentic and assured and stand firm in my beliefs and push back. When I met with my boss and he offered me the promotion, my response was this: "I would love the role and am confident that I will do a great job, as it's perfectly aligned with my long-term career vision. However, if becoming a director, and ultimately an officer, is dependent on me playing golf, then I will have to respectfully decline. I don't think it's fair to force everyone to play at every single meeting, and I think it's wrong to have promotions and career advancement even loosely linked to golf because it undermines our top priority and accountability to our shareholders, which is to generate great business results."

I was prepared for a tough conversation, but instead my boss thanked me for the challenge and said he had not been aware of how this was being perceived. After hearing from me, he now could see that the meetings were not inclusive and were detrimental to building a performance culture. We had a long transparent discussion, and he assured me that whether I played golf or not, the promotion was mine and my career would be based on my merit alone. He also committed to speaking with the leadership team about addressing the lack of inclusivity and performance focus that overemphasizing golf was presenting.

I left the meeting feeling great. Not because I got the promotion but because I got it on my terms, by staying true to my authentic beliefs and by having the self-assuredness to push back. Later, I was part of the group of directors who were tasked to modify the meetings to be more strategy and performance focused and to expand team group activities to promote inclusivity. This experience once again reinforced to me that the right way to achieve my life plan was to pursue my goals while maintaining my authenticity and self-assuredness.

Connecting across Differences

A few years ago, I attended a board of directors meeting in Brazil as part of the management team of a large global company. I was scheduled to give a strategy presentation to the board in the morning, then later that day host the CEO, COO, and a few board members on a visit to one of our manufacturing plants.

The board of directors and company leadership team were comprised of about twenty highly educated, very senior, and successful American businesspeople. I would surmise that each of them was wealthy enough to rank in the top tenth of 1 percent of individual net worth in the world. Conversely, the manufacturing plant that we planned to visit had an employee base earning an average annual salary of only about $5,000 USD. Most of them were high school educated and lived in homes that one might consider favelas or similar. The employees were also a diverse mix of Brazilians and almost none of them spoke English. Clearly, these two groups of people, the board and leadership of the company and the Brazil plant employees, couldn't have been more different.

I presented our strategy to the board in the morning session, and it went very well. I was polished but still authentically myself. I was able to communicate to them in the way they best could understand, the highly educated language of business speak. I was also able to convey confidence because I was self-assured both in my competency of the content and in my ability to connect with them individually and as a group. The CEO and COO approached me after my presentation and said that it was amazing how easily I was able to connect with the board and clearly earn their confidence and respect.

Later that afternoon, we traveled to the manufacturing facility. I knew that the factory employees would be very nervous about this visit from the dignitaries. I wondered if the team members also were curious as to how I would behave. Would I focus my attention on the visiting leadership of the company while on the production floor to further my career progression, or would I do what I normally do when I visit our plants and focus on interacting with our team members?

I could use this as an opportunity to lead the tour myself, since I knew the factory and systems very well and could help the VIPs feel more comfortable in an environment that was pretty foreign to them. This would seem to be a great career move to leverage this rare opportunity to have direct interpersonal connection with the management team and board members of the company to demonstrate my differential leadership and dramatically increase my probability of promotion to executive vice president and C-suite team member.

Or I could stay true to my authentic self and do what I always do, which is to greet every employee like family, speak to them in their own language (I had taught myself Portuguese for this very purpose), listen intently to their stories, and ask what I can do to help them. I knew that our team members were nervous and intimidated by the company leaders touring the facility. It also made sense to me that by focusing my attention on our team members, I could allay their anxiety.

I had a decision to make. When we eventually went on the plant tour, it wasn't a difficult decision for me at all. I told the plant manager and his team to lead the tour with the VIPs and for them to use this as an opportunity to connect with the company leadership team to further their career development. I accompanied them on the tour to help translate and provide context to the VIPs when needed while ensuring that they felt comfortable in the plant. But I also repeatedly ventured away from the tour to greet every team member in Portuguese, hear how they and their families were doing, and demonstrate to them that, to me, they were just as important as the VIP visitors in the top tenth of 1 percent.

I effectively connected interpersonally with both groups even though they were from two completely different worlds, and I was able to do so by being authentic and self-assured.

CHAPTER 13

THE A-ATTITUDES OF LEADERSHIP INTRAPERSONAL TIER

The intrapersonal tier of the A-attitudes of leadership model is comprised of accountability and action. It is built on the foundational tier and leverages the self-awareness and self-belief developed therein to help you operate at the highest levels and reach your full potential. The focus of the intrapersonal tier is to build your capability to be self-inspired to act and to hold yourself accountable to a much higher standard to lead and begin the journey of taking control of your life and your destiny.

FIGURE 13.1: THE A-ATTITUDES OF LEADERSHIP INTRAPERSONAL TIER

Accountability

Accountability is the quality or state of being willingly obligated to accept responsibility or to account for one's actions. This definition infers a past action for which you accept accountability, but with the Destiny Development Delta model, we focus on proactive accountability to take action that allows one to grow, progress, achieve, and strive for excellence. It's about setting goals and targets, making plans to achieve these goals, and adopting process rigor and discipline to hold yourself accountable to execute, iterate, and steadily move forward. Self-accountability is one of the top qualities that I value when hiring and promoting people. Ironically, it is difficult to find people who truly hold themselves accountable.

It is unrealistic to think that everything you do will always work. You must accept that you will have failures. Maintaining the courage to act and hold yourself accountable to a high standard while accepting that you will not get everything right all the time, and viewing the times you fall short as opportunities to learn and grow, is the key. This accountability of viewing every action you take, successful or not, as an opportunity to learn something is the Development Delta core mindset of continuous learning. Several studies have underscored the importance of accountability to overall success. The following are a couple of the key findings from this research:

- As Linda Galindo, author of *The 85% Solution: How Personal Accountability Guarantees Success—No Nonsense, No Excuses*, said, "If you believe that you are at least 85 percent responsible for your success—and that just 15 percent of the success of a project or a day could depend on the way the wind blows—you'll get the results you're looking for."
- A *Forbes* article cited their own research on assessing the business world's most exceptional leaders and indicated that all of them placed in the ninetieth percentile on effectiveness for accountability.

Action

Action is defined as the process of exerting force to do something, typically to move yourself or something else forward, to achieve a goal or address a problem. Individuals following the Destiny Development Delta model will develop the wherewithal to take action, even when faced with uncertainty and risk. The laws of physics are clear—nothing moves unless initiated by a requisite action or force. Therefore, inaction will eventually lead to putting your destiny at risk. Unfortunately, I have seen many people practice inaction repeatedly, even after talking vociferously and at length about the future they want for themselves. This simple physical law may seem obvious, but it is counterintuitive to some, as they think that standing pat or doing nothing is less risky than achieving their destiny. But if you have a genuine life goal that is truly worth pursuing, inaction pushes it further and further out of reach, greatly increasing the likelihood that it will never be attained.

Over the course of my career, being true to my authentic self and assured in my self-belief have inspired me to consistently take action, especially when the outcome was uncertain and the stakes were high, and this has been one of the keys to my success. I believe that if you want to control your destiny, you will need to build the courage to take action. There is a reason why successful entrepreneurs share one unifying quality—fearlessness and the willingness to take big-time risks. Without this quality, they never would have initiated their legacy businesses.

Here is the perspective of one of my mentees, Camilla, regarding the intrapersonal tier:

> I am a strong, authentic woman. With me, what you see is what you get. I am also confident and very self-assured and never hold back on my opinions. But I wasn't holding myself accountable to declare what I wanted in life. This was OK when I was twenty-five but not as a forty-something-year-old married woman with a family. As I started working with Donzel, he coached me on the fact that authenticity and assuredness are really a great

foundation, but I had to use them to hold myself accountable to take the time for myself and my family to think about what I wanted long term. What did I want for my family? What did I want for my career? How important [were] balance and well-being . . . to me on this journey? And most important, he coached me to use my confidence and authenticity to hold myself accountable to act by declaring to others what I wanted. You see, although I was outspoken, I was not so much with my specific career goals, partly because I hadn't really laid out what I wanted because I thought in shorter terms. Donzel helped me to think strategically about myself, to see what my future could be if I wanted it and help me use my self-assuredness to advocate for it. Our family's lives changed shortly thereafter, and importantly to me, I am on the journey to my destiny.

What follows are some personal stories related to the A-attitudes of leadership intrapersonal tier of accountability and action to bring it to life and to illustrate that even when this tier is the focus, it still relies on the foundational tier for support.

Be Accountable to Act for Yourself

Physical fitness was a critical part of my initial life plan almost thirty years ago. I have been keenly aware that I operate most efficiently when I am physically fit and healthy. My ideas are crisper, my problem-solving is sharper, my physical and intellectual endurance is much stronger, I sleep better, and I have greater patience and resilience. In other words, it provides me with the holistic balance and well-being I need to be my best self. However, like many other people, I got off track.

In 1994 when I was twenty-six years old, I allowed my myself to get out of balance and prioritized other things in my life over my fitness. We had a young family I had to help take care of, and we were trying to buy our first home, which put a lot of pressure on me financially to make it happen. Also, as part of my life plan, I had started pursuing my MBA through an accelerated program. If that weren't enough, I had recently become the youngest person ever promoted to the largest and most visible department manager job in the company, which was great, but it put even more pressure on me to prove that I deserved it and was ready. I applied extreme focus on building credibility quickly by working long hours seven days a week to strengthen relationships and to be on top of all issues. Something had to give. To create the bandwidth to manage all of these priorities, I stopped focusing on my health and physical fitness. It wasn't purposeful; it just happened. I kept telling myself that I would get back to it soon, but, of course, I didn't.

After a few years, I had successfully earned my MBA, bought our first home, and then changed companies for another big promotion to accelerate my career trajectory. Then I discovered how far out of balance I had gotten. As part of my preemployment physical to join the new company, I learned some shocking facts about my health. I had gained fifty pounds in two years, ballooning up to 270; had developed high blood pressure; and my knees, which were already problematic from football injuries, had deteriorated more from carrying the excess weight. The new company required additional tests to better gauge the health insurance risk I presented to them before hiring me. Eventually, I was cleared and hired.

You might think that this would have been the wake-up call I needed to get back in balance, but sadly, it was not. We moved our family to a new state, where we bought a new house, and I immersed myself in the new job to, again, gain credibility, build strong relationships, and get up to speed as quickly as possible. I was working even more hours than before. It was another year before I stepped on a scale again and realized that I had gained another forty-five pounds and now weighed 315. This was finally the wake-up call I needed.

My wife was three months pregnant with our third child at the time, and I knew that there was no way I was going to be able to keep up with three young kids at this unhealthy weight. It was time to reassess myself. I referenced my life plan and reaffirmed that I was on track from a career and wealth generation standpoint. But I was clearly way off track from a holistic balance perspective. My well-being was suffering, and I was not bringing my best self to my family every day. I needed to hold myself accountable to get back into balance. I set a goal to lose sixty pounds by the time our third child was born, or ten pounds per month.

At that time, I was pretty much overeating and not exercising at all. Every day, I would eat a full breakfast, a large pizza for lunch, and two large servings of dinner and dessert. I theorized that if I simply cut the size of my meals in half by changing to a piece of fruit for breakfast, a salad with no dressing for lunch, one normal serving for dinner and no dessert, and exercise thirty minutes a day seven days per week, I could lose the weight. The key for me was to take action to start, then hold myself accountable to stay with it. To ensure that I made this happen, I decided to give up an hour of sleep by getting up at four thirty to exercise, thus not taking time away from family, school, or work. I also put a picture of my wife and kids on the stair stepper to remind myself every morning who was counting on me to be healthy. I developed a template to track my compliance and progress and came up with little rewards at the end of the week for when I successfully hit my goals.

With this plan in place, I lost one hundred pounds in four months, two months before my daughter Joanell was born. I beat my original goal by thirty pounds in two fewer months. At 215 pounds, I didn't feel quite myself, so I decided to gain ten pounds back. At 225, I felt really great. The mental sharpness came back. The creativity came back. The problem-solving came back. The increased patience came back. Not that I had totally lost it when I was overweight, but the extremely high-functioning levels I had before I gained all that weight returned. And importantly, my sense of holistic balance and well-being returned as well.

Since then, I have maintained my weight, health, fitness, well-being, and balance by continuing to reaffirm to myself who I am, remind myself what is important to me, reference my authentic life plan, and hold myself accountable to take and sustain the action required to control my life and make my destiny happen.

Accountability and Action to Break the Glass Ceiling

In 2012, I became vice president of the international operations of a large global manufacturing company. At the time, we had close to forty operations sites outside the United States. One of the first things that stood out to me was that many of our international factories had a higher percentage of female workers than our US plants, and in many cases, women were the majority. But ironically, none of our international plants were led or managed by women while several were in the US. I later discovered that not only did we not have any women factory managers internationally at the time, to the best that I could verify, but also we had never had a single woman managing a factory outside the US. It seemed to me that we had a real or perceived glass ceiling in our international operations sites for women.

Our lack of female factory managers was not a question of talent availability, as we had several capable women in our organization across multiple geographies. Instead, it was more a question of whether senior leadership would hold itself accountable to take action and make this a priority. Clearly, this was an indictment on leadership, but now I was senior leadership. I was accountable to take action. What was I going to do about it?

I worked with our leadership teams across all geographic regions to develop a plan to identify our top female operations leaders and provide them with accelerated development to prepare them to be factory managers in short order. Not surprisingly, all of them were already on our top talent list, but there had never been accountable action dedicated to addressing what had been a lack of committed coaching, mentoring, and sponsorship. We were going to fix that and also challenge and stretch them by providing greater breadth of leadership accountability. We established measurable milestones to monitor their progress and hold their managers accountable to ensure they stayed on track. I set up monthly one-to-one meetings with each of them to build their capability and confidence. I committed to being their coach and mentor and to provide them with a safe space to ask questions, get advice, and seek support. I also assured them that I was accountable for their advancement and would personally sponsor and advocate for their promotions.

Within two years, we went from zero female plant managers in our international facilities to five spread across three continents. A few years later, our transformation continued, as 50 percent of our regional supply chain directors, who are responsible for end-to-end operations across multiple countries, were women. I took accountability to make sure that we were not the chameleon that simply changed colors but instead the caterpillar that permanently transformed into a beautiful butterfly.

CHAPTER 14

THE A-ATTITUDES OF LEADERSHIP INTERPERSONAL TIER

The interpersonal tier of the A-attitudes of leadership model is comprised of accessibility and adoration. The focus of this tier is on building your capability to inspire, lead, influence, and engage others to help achieve your objectives but also for you to help them achieve theirs. It is supported by both the foundational tier and the intrapersonal tier because one must leverage authenticity, assuredness, and accountability to take action to proactively develop strategic externally facing interactions.

FIGURE 14.1: THE A-ATTITUDES OF LEADERSHIP INTERPERSONAL TIER

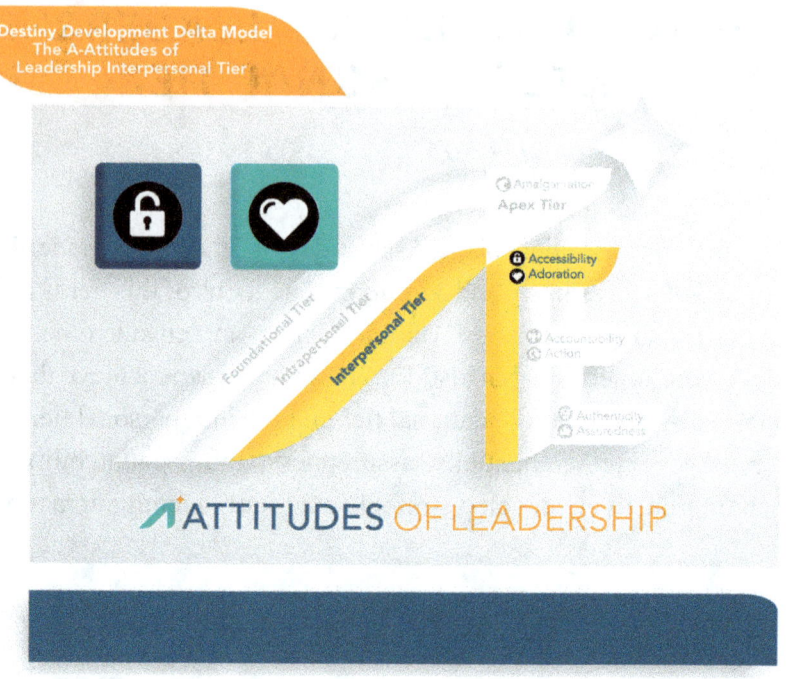

Accessibility

Accessibility is defined as reachable, attainable, and approachable. It is characterized by leaders who unlock themselves to be extremely available, welcoming, friendly, pleasant, and easy to talk to. But truly accessible leaders don't wait for people to approach them; they proactively go to the people to demonstrate their openness. This is a critical enabler of the Destiny Development Delta model because it builds the capability for creating the support networks you will need to take control of your life and destiny. Striving for success on your own rarely yields breakthrough results. To achieve something great, we all need and help from a strong network of passionate supporters.

Through the A-attitudes of leadership model, you will develop the capability not only to unlock your accessibility but also to proactively cultivate and build the support networks you will need with authentic and assured interpersonal effectiveness and influence. According to the Institute of Behavioral and Applied Management article "Testing the Relationship between Interpersonal Political Skills, Altruism, Leadership Success and Effectiveness: A Multilevel Model" by Jennifer A. Moss and John E. Barbuto, the authors concluded that "a leader's interpersonal influence significantly impacts ratings of effectiveness . . . [and] that those who are skilled at networking within an organization are more successful."

Remember that in the Destiny Development Delta model, you are the leader of your life, and to take control of your destiny, you must view yourself as a leader.

Adoration

Adoration is defined as love and respect for others. As I stated earlier, the interpersonal tier focuses on building your capability to inspire, lead, influence, and engage others to help achieve your objectives but also for you to help them achieve theirs. I believe that to truly engage and, more importantly, inspire people, one must have genuine adoration for them. Prioritizing and developing adoration as core to your personal transformation is critically important, especially in recruiting passionate supporters to help you achieve your life plan. However, it is also one of the hardest things to do and will rely heavily on your authenticity and assuredness to hold yourself accountable to take action with courage and resolve. Love is tough and hard, not weak, while hate and ambivalence are easy. Sachin Tendulkar, who is widely regarded as the greatest cricketer of all time, is also a philanthropist and national hero in India, and he once said about love, "It is easy to hate, and it is difficult to love. This is how the whole scheme of things works. All good things are difficult to achieve; and bad things are very easy to get."

To build a strong and diverse network of supporters, you must have the courage, passion, and drive to engage with those outside your comfort zone. Dr. Martin Luther King Jr. once said, "Love is the only force capable of transforming an enemy into friend." People tend to gravitate to those they have more similarities with and away from those with whom they have less in common. Dr. Maya Angelou once wrote on Facebook, "Love recognizes no barriers. It jumps hurdles, leaps fences, penetrates walls to arrive at its destination full of hope." By actively engaging with those who are different from us, foreign to us, or unknown to us, we build our ability to connect socially, culturally, and interpersonally with empathy that will change our authentic perspective. In addition, engaging with diverse people invariably introduces valuable new perspectives, stretching our learning capacity and increasing our mental sharpness.

According to the article "How Diversity Makes Us Smarter" by Katherine W. Phillips, "It seems obvious that a group of people with diverse individual expertise would be better than a homogeneous group at solving complex, nonroutine problems. It is less obvious that social diversity should work in the same way—yet the science shows that it does. This is not only because people with different backgrounds bring new information. Simply interacting with individuals who are different forces group members to prepare better, to anticipate alternative viewpoints and to expect that reaching consensus will take effort."

Accessibility is enhanced by adoration, powerfully amplifying it, when adoration is authentic and altruistic in its motives. I believe in the inherent goodness of people, and I see it as my duty as a leader to find that goodness, inspire it to emerge from those I interact with, and help bring about positive well-being for them. Dr. Martin Luther King Jr. also said, "Every man must decide whether he will walk in the light of creative altruism or in the darkness of destructive selfishness." I know that by being accessible and by showing adoration, I am nurturing my own well-being and creating deep connections for building a passionate and diverse network of supporters.

According to the previously referenced article by Jennifer A. Moss and John E. Barbuto, the authors also concluded that "interpersonal influence was positively related to effectiveness, and networking ability was positively related to both effectiveness and success. In addition, altruism enhanced the relationship between social astuteness and effectiveness and has a direct impact on leadership effectiveness." Again, I remind you that in the Destiny Development Delta model, references to leadership apply to you, because you are the leader of your life, and to take control of your destiny, you must view yourself as a leader.

My commitment to holding myself accountable to act with true accessibility and adoration has had a major role in my life success and in my continued progressive pursuit of my ultimate life goals. I can honestly say that I have spent at least 60 percent of my professional time throughout my career being truly accessible to people in my radius through direct one-to-one interpersonal connection. I have continually expanded my network radius by always being accessible. I estimate that over the course of my career, I have had one-to-one meetings with at least ten thousand different people across thirty different countries. In terms of time, I estimate that over the course of my career, I have invested more than fifty thousand hours in one-to-one meetings with others, whether in a field location, on the production floor, off-site, in offices, or virtually. If I included team meetings and group discussions focused on relationship and team building, coaching, and inspiring, excluding business-focused meetings, then the overall time investment in accessibility would be about 90 percent of my time, or greater than seventy-five thousand hours over the course of my career. And this is only counting my professional career, not the time I have invested in accessibility outside of work in community engagement and leadership, coaching, and mentoring; if I added those, it would be an additional thirty thousand hours. That's more than one hundred thousand hours of accessibility, demonstrating adoration, and advocating for, coaching, and inspiring people.

Here is the perspective of Sidharth, one of my mentees, regarding the interpersonal tier:

> Donzel's role modeling of accessibility and adoration have been one of the most impactful leadership lessons of my entire working life. His coaching of how to leverage authenticity to serve a higher

purpose inspires me and everyone else. It is about being there for people and caring for people. It generates a beacon of hope and positive action during even the most difficult times. When times were very tough for me, and I questioned my leadership, I remember Donzel telling me, *What if you weren't here?* That would inspire me to let my genuine care come through more. It inspires me to give of myself more. And honestly, the more I care for others and give to others, I have seen how much better our team has performed. And the more fulfilled our team members say they are, the more I feel that I am fulfilled.

The following are some stories to bring to life the A-attitudes of leadership interpersonal tier of accessibility and adoration and to illustrate that even when this tier is the focus, it still relies on both the intrapersonal tier and the foundational tier for support.

Never Underestimate the Power of Adoration and Accessibility

Here is an example of adoration and accessibility having an impact that I didn't see coming. I had recently joined a large manufacturing company as the production director. Once I arrived, I spent a lot of time on the production floor and in the maintenance shop across all three shifts. I focused on getting to know everyone in our organization, including some three hundred operators and one hundred maintenance technicians.

There was a second-shift maintenance technician named Daniel who was especially difficult to get to know. Every time that I would see him on the production floor or come into the maintenance shop to speak to him, he would barely engage, and when he did, it was usually with an odd comment. After a while, a few of the technicians and supervisors told me to ignore Daniel because he was weird. I told them that we should not prejudge people and that he may just be an introvert who now feels more isolated because he knows what they all think and say about him. They all said, "You'll see." I told them that I guess I would see because I would continue to work to get to know Daniel.

I made efforts to connect with Daniel and build some kind of a relationship. I made some slight progress, as he started to respond by telling me his complaints about his job and his workmates. I would always listen intently to Daniel and follow up on his complaints. I would also push back when I had researched his complaints and knew that he didn't have a complete picture or was prejudging things or people himself. Anytime I pushed back on Daniel, he didn't like it and would hurriedly walk away. But after a while, we could have a somewhat productive conversation, and if something came up about which we didn't agree, he would at least stay and then say he would think about it. But I never felt that Daniel really trusted me. He always kept me at arm's length.

Then one day while I was in my office meeting with another team member, someone banged on my door and said there had been a fight. It was a dangerous situation, and we had to evacuate the plant. He said, "The fire department and police are here, and one of the guys involved in the fight is holed up inside the locker room and won't come out. This guy says the only person he'll talk to is you. I think it's Daniel from maintenance."

Once outside, I spoke to the police officers, and they confirmed that it was Daniel inside and that he would speak only to me. They also said that they didn't know if Daniel was armed and that because he was not talking to them, they would have to assume he was. They then told me that if Daniel did not peacefully surrender, SWAT would go in and extract him using deadly force, if necessary. At that moment, it became very clear to me how critical this situation was. Daniel's safety and possibly his life now depended on the strength of our relationship and on me being able to talk him into surrendering.

They called Daniel on the locker-room phone and put me on to speak to him. I said, "Hello, Daniel. What's going on, my friend? You asked to talk to me?" When Daniel replied, I could hear the emotional strain in his voice. He said, "Donzel, I'm scared. I don't want to come out. No one likes me, and everyone is against me. You're the only person I trust. Please tell me what to do."

I responded, "Daniel, everyone is not against you. I'm your friend, and I'm here for you. I think it's best that you come out now. It doesn't matter what happened. All that matters now is that you're safe and that you remain safe to go back home to your family."

"OK," Daniel replied. "If you say I should come out, then I'll come out. But please meet me at the door and walk with me. I don't think I can do it alone." I met Daniel at the door and immediately hugged him. He buried his head in my shoulder, then started crying and repeating, "I'm sorry. I'm sorry."

We began walking, and then I felt his legs give way. I yelled to the police and EMTs that we needed medical assistance immediately because Daniel was collapsing. The EMTs were able to get Daniel on a gurney, but he would not release me from his embrace. He kept saying, "Donzel, you're the only person I trust here. You're the only one who cares. Please stay with me." After about ten minutes, I convinced Daniel that it was OK to let me go so that the ambulance could take him to the hospital and that I would meet them there.

As I drove to the hospital, the gravity of what had just happened hit me. I had held myself accountable to be accessible to Daniel and had taken action to show him authentic adoration, even when it appeared to not have much impact. But because of my assured belief and persistence, I had built such a strong relationship with Daniel that we successfully navigated a critically dangerous situation and possibly saved his life.

Building a Global Family

It has always been part of my life plan to build a large global network. Growing up in Key West, I was exposed to people from all over the world. I believe in the power of diversity and had developed a real affinity and curiosity for connecting with people whose home countries and cultures were different from mine and who may look, think, and have varying beliefs. The legendary writer Mark Twain famously said, "Travel is fatal to prejudice," and I believe in this literally and figuratively. Being both physically and mentally accessible and having true adoration for learning allows us to connect differentially across boundaries not only to defeat ignorance but also to build powerful relationships. Additionally, it accelerates the expansion of our knowledge by exposing us to different perspectives, cultures, histories, and beliefs to fully maximize personal growth and empathy.

To build a large global network, I realized that it required me to connect and establish real relationships with anyone from anywhere. To do this, I leveraged my authenticity, self-assuredness, and accountability to take action and immerse myself wherever I was to be fully present with whomever I was with. I would focus on recognizing and valuing each person individually, as in the South African greeting *Sawubona*, which means "I see you fully and regard you as a human being." For me, one of the truest tests of my accessibility and adoration is connecting across geographic, language, and cultural barriers and still conveying the feeling of *Sawubona*.

For example, when I would visit our teams in different parts of the world, I would always take the time to regard each person as if they were family. I wanted our teams to feel my adoration for them as individuals, so I greeted them in their language accompanied by a warm hug.

I remember the first time I planned to visit China. Several American colleagues told me that I should not treat the Chinese people the same way I treated everyone else because it was against their culture to hug, and it would be impossible for me to explain anything to them because they don't speak English. I didn't listen to this nonsense because people are people. I knew that I didn't have to speak Mandarin perfectly or they English to make them feel like they mattered. This wasn't a complicated theory or concept. It was simply about connecting with people, and I was assured that my authentic accessibility and adoration would translate across any barriers.

Before I arrived, I studied Chinese culture, including the importance of names and how they convey a significant meaning from parents and tell the story and history of the family. Most Westerners find it difficult to pronounce Chinese names (and the names of people from other Asian countries), so quite often a person from an Asian country working for a multinational will adopt an English name to acquiesce. For me to follow this convention would not demonstrate adoration. Having the authenticity and assuredness to greet people in their language and the accountability to take action and learn to pronounce their real names correctly would demonstrate my respect and honor for them.

I arrived in Shanghai three days early to immerse myself in the culture and learn how to pronounce greetings and names. I even took the extraordinary step of adopting a Chinese name to accommodate them and demonstrate just how much they mattered and how important respecting their culture was to me. In my view, this was true *Sawubona* because it would send a message to each person: "I see you, you are a person, you matter, and so does your history and culture."

When I met with our team members for the first time, I introduced myself in Mandarin and shared my Chinese name. I then asked for their Chinese names, and I pronounced them correctly (after a few tries). This was a shocking but pleasant surprise to everyone. I also gave each person a very sincere and warm hug. They were caught off guard when I greeted them with an embrace. Many of them froze and were simply speechless. When I left a few hours later, I was proud that I was authentic and demonstrated true accessibility and adoration, but I questioned whether it was effective.

A few months later, during my second visit, I received a very clear answer. The visit that had taken two hours just a few months before now took six hours, because those same team members who froze and were speechless the last time we met now lined up to greet me in Mandarin and welcome me by my Chinese name. They also wanted to give me updates on their families and their lives, teach me more about Chinese culture, and, most importantly, get their hug.

This is a representative example of all my visits with our teams around the world. Visits that were usually one to two hours for other leaders became six to eight hours for me, with many extending multiple days at locations with large team member populations. This was the same whether it was China, South Korea and other parts of the Far East, Australia, India, the UAE, France, Greece (Hellas), Spain, the UK, Argentina, Brazil, Canada, or Mexico. I didn't just create connections; I established deep relationships that endure almost fifteen years later. I began with a goal of building a global network, but because of my authentic accessibility and adoration, I built a global family.

CHAPTER 15

THE A-ATTITUDES OF LEADERSHIP APEX TIER

The apex tier represents the culmination of the A-attitudes of leadership development model. Its focus is the summation of all tiers creating a holistic personal transformation that is greater than the simple sum of its parts.

FIGURE 15.1: THE A-ATTITUDES OF LEADERSHIP APEX TIER

Amalgamation

The apex tier is comprised of amalgamation, which represents the distinct new transcendent skill set that has been formed through the synergistic summation of the A-attitudes of leadership tiers. This culmination of personal development ensures that the newly transformed individual is ready for integration with the iLEAD change model in milestone 2 of the Destiny Development Delta model. The apex tier is validation that through self-awareness and the A-attitudes of leadership, you are effectively prepared to take control of your life and relentlessly make your destiny happen.

Here is what my mentee Michael said relative to amalgamation:

> The A-attitudes of leadership have taught me a lot about myself. They also taught me what it will take for me to be happy and comfortable in my life. For me, if I find holistic balance in my life where I am comfortable in my personal life, work life, and social life, I will be a much happier human overall. If I make sure to take care of myself and pay attention to my personal well-being, then I will make sure that I am not only healthy emotionally but also physically. I want to get into a routine of working out and eating right, and once I can do that, I think my personal well-being will become much better than it is now. In order to get to the point where I want to be, I will need to work hard at tackling a few stress points in my life. The A-attitudes of leadership are helping me take control of my compulsiveness and manage my stress. With this, I will be much happier and much better suited to take control of my own destiny.

The following are some personal stories to bring amalgamation of all the A-attitudes of leadership to life.

My A-Attitudes of Leadership Role Models

A few years ago, I spoke at a leadership conference as part of a panel of executives to discuss what defines great leadership. The first question was this: "If you all are our leadership role models, can you tell us who were yours?" One CEO said the late US Senator Paul Wellstone because he was an inspirational progressive leader who died before his time. A COO said Steve Jobs because he led breakthrough innovation and invention. A CFO said Warren Buffett because he is the financial wizard of our time. When it came to me, I said that the three previously mentioned people certainly could be considered great leaders. But in my opinion, I have three of the greatest leaders of all time as my role models: my great-grandmother, my grandmother, and my mother. But I told them that for the sake of time, I would speak specifically about my great-grandmother and my grandmother.

My great-grandmother, Vera Butler, whom we affectionately called Ma' Vera, lived to be 107 years old and was the strongest person I ever knew. She was nearly eighty when I was born but immediately started babysitting me. As I grew, I remember becoming aware that she was older, but I never saw her as elderly because she was so commanding and forceful with her will and blunt with her opinions. She never drove a car; instead, she walked everywhere, and no one ever dared bother her. In fact, she wasn't afraid of anything or anyone. She was extremely self-assured.

I learned many valuable life lessons from her that I carry with me today. She taught me the value of education, because she never had the opportunity to formally finish hers (she had to quit school in the sixth grade to start working). Every day, she would teach my cousins and me math lessons on the school board, as she called it, which was a two-by-two piece of plywood on which she had written out the times table. She would tell us how much things had changed since she was a little girl and how her future had been extremely limited based on her race and gender but that we now had the chance to do things she couldn't have imagined if we focused on education and worked hard.

She taught me the importance of understanding the value of money and the discipline of frugality, saving and protecting your assets. She'd owned her own home since at least 1934, an incredible feat at the time, and was meticulous about its upkeep and maintenance. Very prudently, she spent money only on true necessities. If anyone, no matter who, tried to touch or move her purse, she would immediately slap their hand. Most importantly, she taught me that there are no excuses. She would often tell me, "No one is better than you, but you are not better than anyone. It's about who works harder."

My grandmother Yvonne Allen, whom we affectionately called Mama Yvonne, also ended her formal education in middle school, quitting in her teens to enter the labor force like her mother, Ma' Vera, did, working as a maid for more than forty years. I didn't spend as much time with her as I did with Ma' Vera because she was still working when I was a child. She raised nine children, and she and my grandfather saved all the pennies they had. Through her determination, courage, and faith, they were able to buy their first home in 1965. Again, this was an incredible feat for a maid and a laborer at that time.

I remember being amazed by how hard she worked. She believed that if you're going to do a job, then you should hold yourself accountable to do it the right way, the best way, even if that is the hardest way. For example, when she mopped the floors both in her own home and where she worked, she always cleaned by hand, not with a mop, inch by inch on her elbows and knees, causing them to always be dark and calloused.

She believed that no matter what you do, you should have pride in your work, but it should not determine who you are. She taught me that whether you are a wet nurse, a maid, a store owner, the mayor, or an executive at a big company, it's not your job that defines you; it's your authentic character.

Neither Mama Yvonne nor Ma' Vera were highly educated, and both held jobs that many would consider among the lowest in a class-driven society. But nevertheless, they had incredible self-value, self-worth, and spiritual well-being. Because of their authenticity and self-assuredness, they never let their job titles, education, or anyone's perceptions or prejudgments define them. They held themselves accountable to a higher standard and modeled, trained, and taught us to be determined, resilient, and self-assured. They took action as the leaders in our family, in the church, and in the community, and they were pillars of strength for everyone when things were tough. They were accessible and showed compassion and love to anyone who required help, sharing what little they had with those in need and treating them like family.

When I reflect on who I am today and why, it's clear to me that it was the lessons of the A-attitudes of leadership that I gained from them that helped shape me.

- *Authenticity and assuredness:* Never let any person, group, organization, or company define who you are. Develop self-agency. Believe in yourself and be a leader. They stood tall no matter what people thought of them. They had two of the lowest-level jobs in their society, but they did not let that define them. Instead, their strength, courage, and determination did.
- *Accessibility and adoration:* Treat people the way they need to be treated, like your family. Always be willing to help, support, and stand up for others who can't stand up for themselves.
- *Action and accountability:* No one is better than you, but you are no better than anyone else. The difference is how much you hold yourself accountable to work hard. They didn't have the chance to focus on education and continuous learning, but I did, and if I could combine those with the tremendous work ethic and determination they had, I could accomplish anything. Nothing could stop me from striving to be the best and controlling my destiny.

The A-Attitudes of Leadership Guide the Way to Family

Another great example of how the A-attitudes of leadership guide the way occurred during my visit to India in December 2019. This was my sixth trip to India and my second that year. A major objective this time was to visit our team in Maharashtra state, and the highlight for me, as always, was the facility tour to check overall progress and, most importantly, spend time interacting with the team members. As I mentioned in an earlier story, we used to plan two hours for my tours of our facilities, but over the years, we learned to expect a full day to allow me to personally connect with every team member, giving them my full attention. I knew almost all of our five hundred team members well because of my previous visits and in-depth conversations with them, so it was like reuniting with family members whenever I would come back.

During my prior visit six months earlier, I stopped at Viraj's station and asked about his family and farm. Viraj had previously told me about his farm and how it not only provided extra income and allowed him to be an entrepreneur but also how it was a significant part of Indian family culture. I knew that his family and his farm were important to him. He told me that his family was fine and that his farm was doing well and that he would be proud if I would come see it. I told him that I would do so on my next visit.

Fast-forward to December 2019. We were midway through the facility tour when I saw Viraj. He showed me all the great projects he and his team had completed over the last six months. I told him that they had made fantastic progress, and I was very proud of them. He thanked me and then asked if I was still coming to visit his farm. I immediately remembered the promise I made and then, to my chagrin, realized I had not added the farm visit to the already tight agenda. I now had a tough decision to make. For me to keep my word and go to his farm, we would have to modify the agenda and risk missing my flight back home, as the drive from the facility to Mumbai International Airport could range anywhere from four to eight hours depending on traffic and road conditions following monsoon season. If we missed this flight, we would have to stay in India at least one additional day.

Clearly, Viraj had been planning for this, and I didn't want to let him down. I quickly thought through the A-attitudes of leadership model. I considered the fact that demonstrating authentic adoration and accessibility is not about when it is convenient for me but when it supports and honors others. Additionally, I had the self-assuredness to recognize that this was not only a way to honor Viraj but also a true learning and growth opportunity for me. Finally, I had made a promise to Viraj, and I wanted to hold myself accountable to make it happen. I took action and decided to go to the farm, taking the risk that I might miss my flight home.

We had an amazing visit at the farm. Viraj showed us where each crop is grown, explained the rotations, and provided samples. He shared the business model for his farm, described the split between domestic and export sales, and presented his vision for growth. I was very impressed with his strategic approach to the farm's long-term viability. And because things were progressing smoothly, it appeared that we shouldn't have a problem making the flight. But Viraj had a surprise for us.

As soon as the farm visit was complete, Viraj invited us to his home. I was not expecting this and realized that if I accepted, we would probably miss our flight, but I could see how important this was to Viraj, and my commitment to accessibility and adoration took over. About twenty minutes later, we arrived at Viraj's home, where his mother, father, wife, six-year-old daughter, two-year-old son, six-month-old daughter, brother, sister-in-law, niece, and nephew all greeted us with gifts of traditional village hats and long scarves. They invited us to sit down as honored guests and explained the significance of the gifts to their culture.

Viraj then said that he wanted to make sure that I got to meet those who support and count on him at home, his family, but more importantly he wanted them to meet the executive from the US who inspires, engages, and treats him like someone who truly matters. He said, "Mr. Donzel is now a member of our family."

I felt so very humbled and honored at that moment that I didn't care if we missed our flight and had to stay for an additional three days. I said, "Viraj, you said it is your honor to host me in your home because I inspire you and care for you, but the truth is that I am the one who is most honored and inspired to be here and be welcomed as part of your family."

It was truly a moving experience, one that was unexpected and one that you cannot buy. Because I leveraged the A-attitudes of leadership to guide my way, I not only dramatically expanded my perspective but also gained a whole new family in Maharashtra, India, more than eight thousand miles away from my home. Clearly, this was good karma because I still got to the airport in time to make my flight as scheduled.

A few years later, Viraj's declaration that I was part of his family manifested in some incredible actions. During the global COVID-19 pandemic, Viraj was one of the team members who stepped up to help develop and implement standardized social distancing practices to safely continue our operations with minimal disruption while many peer companies were shut down by the government for extended periods. The following year, there was unrest in our facility caused by a few bad actors attempting to take over leadership and potentially disrupt the operation. Viraj once again stepped up and led an effort to stop this takeover and ensure that rational leadership remained in place. In both instances, when asked by leadership and other team members why he took action at these critically important moments, Viraj said, "Because help was needed and Donzel is our leader, but he is also my friend and my family, and I won't let this happen to him. This is how you support family."

CHAPTER 16

THE A-ATTITUDES OF LEADERSHIP DEVELOPMENT MODELS AND PROCESSES

Focused and personalized A-attitudes of leadership coaching and development are required to fully build the capability necessary to take and sustain control of one's destiny. Next are a few of the development models and processes, in abbreviated form, that are leveraged to support this development. The full suite of proprietary A-attitudes of leadership models, processes, and tools are available through consultation with Destiny Development Delta LLC.

THE PERSON IN THE GLASS MODEL

The person in the glass model is the first A-attitudes of leadership development model and as such appropriately targets the first two tiers. It is most influential and impactful at the foundational tier, specifically with authenticity, because it continually forces you to confront whether you are being true to yourself. And because assuredness is strongly dependent on authenticity, this model tests your resolve and confidence in yourself as well. The person in the glass model also affects the intrapersonal tier, as it tests your ability to hold yourself accountable over time and take action to change if you notice you are veering off course. The following is the story of how this model was first introduced to me, which was integral to my development and ultimately resulted in the model's creation.

As mentioned in a prior chapter, I initially transitioned into people leadership very early in my career due to union employees using their leverage to influence senior management to promote me because they felt I was the only one who actually cared about and listened to them. One of the key members of the group who made this happen was Will. He was in his early sixties at the time and had more than forty years of seniority at the company. Will was a soft-spoken man of few words, so when he did decide to say something, I knew that it must be important and that I should listen intently.

A few weeks after I was promoted, Will asked if we could meet in my office. He told me that he was one of the people who started the movement to get me promoted. He said that in his forty years working there, he had never experienced a leader as caring and inspirational. But then he became more serious. "But you are also very young, and I'm afraid that you'll get sucked into the habits of all the other managers and eventually drift away from what makes you special. I got you this framed poem to help you always remember who you are and what got you here." Will held up a framed poem called "The Man in the Glass," which I later learned isn't credited to a known author. I modified the title to "The Person in the Glass," so it reads a little differently from when Will gave it to me, but the meaning is still the same.

The Person in the Glass

When you get what you want in your struggle for self
and the world makes you king or queen for a day
Just go to the mirror and look at yourself
and see what that person has to say

For it isn't your father, mother, husband, or wife
whose judgment upon you must pass
The person whose verdict counts the most in your life
is the one staring back from the glass

Some people may say that you're honest and great,
a wonderful gal or guy
But the person in the glass says you're only a fake
if you can't look them straight in the eye
Please the one in the glass, never mind all the rest
for you're together clear to the end
And you've passed your most dangerous and difficult test
if the person in the glass is still your friend

You may fool the whole world down the pathway
of life and get pats on the back as you pass
But your final reward will be heartaches and
tears if you've cheated the person in the glass.

Will instructed that I keep this poem with me and that whenever I feel like I'm drifting off-center, read it to test myself. However, I went a step further than Will suggested. I kept the poem next to my computer monitor so that I would see it and read it almost every day. It has been more than thirty years since Will gave me that poem, and I have kept it with me through three changes of companies, fifteen different offices, and six interstate moves. Through all of that change, "The Man in the Glass" has changed only once, when I modified it to "The Person in the Glass." But it has not changed in terms of its critical importance to me and the commitment it represents to myself to always be the authentic Donzel. Four-time NBA MVP, entrepreneur, and outspoken social justice activist LeBron James said, "Commitment is a big part of what I am and what I believe. How committed are you to winning? How committed are you to being a good friend? To being trustworthy? To being successful? How committed are you to being a good father, a good teammate, a good role model? There's that moment every morning when you look in the mirror: Are you committed, or are you not?"

Ultimately, the A-attitudes of leadership model depends on the strength of the foundational tier, authenticity and assuredness. Only you know if you are true to yourself. Leverage the person in the glass for your ongoing accountability assessment to ensure that your authenticity and assuredness stay centered. It may seem like a simple, silly little poem, but, for me, it's powerful because it clearly creates the self-conscious accountability to maintain my authenticity and assuredness. I never forget that the "Donzel in the Glass" is watching me. Figure 16.1 shows the person in the glass model with its recommended steps.

FIGURE 16.1: THE A-ATTITUDES OF LEADERSHIP THE PERSON IN THE GLASS MODEL

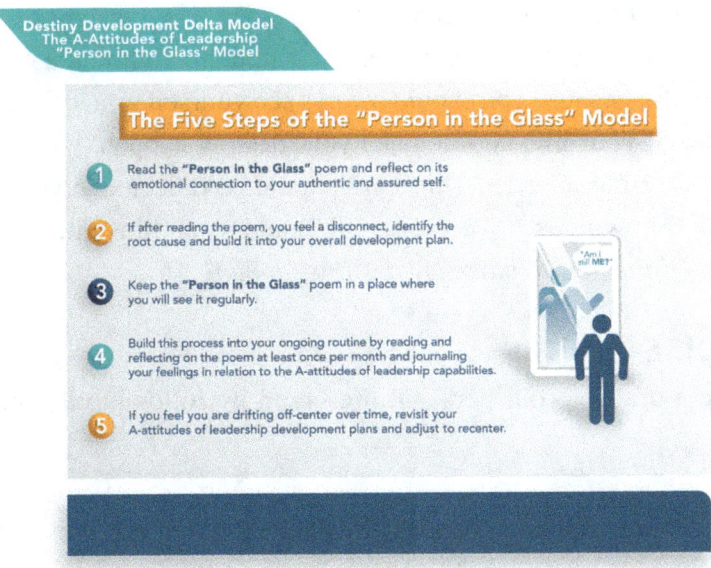

Pause here and follow the first two steps of the model by reading "The Person in the Glass" and then reflect on how it makes you feel and why.

THE A-ATTITUDES OF LEADERSHIP LIFE BRAND DEVELOPMENT PROCESS

The life brand development process is designed to help you visually embody your authentic and assured self as a personal brand. It helps build all the A-attitudes of leadership, starting with the foundational tier because, similar to the person in the glass model, it forces you to confront whether you are being true to yourself by putting into words what you believe you are all about and/or what you aspire to be. It then leverages the intrapersonal tier by testing your ability to hold yourself accountable and take action to live up to your brand. Finally, it uses the interpersonal tier by requiring you to test your brand with others and assess whether they are inspired and engaged. If you are authentic and assured when you share your brand, you will feel energized and reinforced by the inspiration you sense in them. If it is disingenuous, you will not.

It is important to note that as you consider your brand, remember that it doesn't matter whether you are a leader or a manager or whether you do not work outside the home, are a student, an artist, a cashier, or anything else because you should always see yourself as a leader. You are the leader of your life, and to make your destiny happen, you must start to see yourself as a leader. This spirit should be reflected in your brand.

The following is my personal life brand as an illustrative example: *Strive to be the best to make my destiny happen!*

EXERCISE

Develop a draft of your personal life brand by following the steps outlined next.

1. Reflect on the A-attitudes of leadership and write down two to three words for each tier representing your
   a. authenticity and assuredness,
   b. accountability and action,
   c. accessibility and adoration, and
   d. amalgamation and life philosophy.
2. Write two to three words that best represent the message you want to send with your personal brand.
3. Find the themes in all the words you've written and narrow down the list to the five to seven words that are most representative of who you are now and who you want to become.
4. Craft one sentence that integrates the themes into a coherent and inspirational personal brand message.
5. Pressure test by reading "The Person in the Glass" with your brand in mind, and then ask yourself: Am I inspired by this? If you don't feel a sense of pride and inspiration when you say it, continue refining until you do.

CHAPTER 17

HOLISTIC BALANCE AND PERSONAL WELL-BEING DEVELOPMENT

The objective of the intense focus on the A-attitudes of leadership model is ultimately to build inner strength to take control of your destiny, persevere, and sustain it through the challenges of life. This inner strength comes in the form of holistic balance and personal well-being.

HOLISTIC BALANCE

Holistic balance is the ability to achieve and maintain equilibrium across the mind, heart, body, and spirit and is focused on ensuring that all aspects that affect your overall well-being have adequate focus, structure, and attention to stay balanced. When the storms of life come your way and you are facing heavy headwinds, crosswinds, and even tailwinds, all of these can easily knock you off course and out of balance. The chances of being able to sustain, persevere, and come through the storm even stronger than before are greatly improved if you have and continually improve holistic balance. If one area is overdeveloped at the expense of other critical areas, you might be fine if the weather is calm, but as soon as the wind changes, the imbalance is exposed, making it almost impossible to stay on course and sustain healthy control over your life and destiny.

PERSONAL WELL-BEING

Personal well-being is a continuous measure of your state of happiness, contentment with life, and feeling of positive growth. It is about deep emotional self-insight that allows you to fully and truly be in touch with, know, and love yourself. It's also about your ability to recognize when your well-being is suffering and to make the appropriate adjustment to stay on track. It is your personal self-righting ability when the winds of distraction, disappointment, and disillusionment blow you off course.

Personal well-being and holistic balance are directly correlated in that if one is compromised, then the other will be negatively affected. Both can also influence people around us, either lifting them up or dragging them down.

HOLISTIC BALANCE AND PERSONAL WELL-BEING MODEL

The model shown in figure 17.1 illustrates our ability to create an ongoing state of holistic balance and personal well-being. The A-attitudes of leadership concept and the self-awareness it develops underpins the core of the model surrounding and connecting the mind, heart, body, and spirit because all tiers are designed to support both holistic balance and personal well-being. There are three additional factors that are external to the mind, heart, body, and spirit but that can critically influence them and have a significant effect on holistic balance and personal well-being. These three—physical intelligence, financial focus, and mental sharpness—complete the model. Building capability and actively managing these are essential to your transformation.

FIGURE 17.1: HOLISTIC BALANCE AND PERSONAL WELL-BEING MODEL

Physical intelligence is the practical application of the knowledge that your physical condition directly affects your emotional, mental, and spiritual health. I purposefully use the word *intelligence* instead of *fitness* because it's about developing the capacity and conviction to consistently apply this knowledge to stay active, exercise regularly, and maintain a healthy lifestyle to achieve the balance necessary to maintain authenticity and assuredness, consistently take action and hold yourself accountable, and maintain the positive energy needed to be accessible and show adoration. Developing and applying physical intelligence as a means and process for transformation is integral to building the foundation required to make your destiny happen. Research shows the positive correlation between regular exercise and improved productivity and, more importantly, between holistic balance and personal well-being. I can also personally attest that it has been integral to my life success.

For physical intelligence to work, *you* must recognize that it is the practical application of the knowledge, that it is about *your* physical condition and what works best for *you* to achieve healthy physical balance. Everyone is different, and your definition of the variables that make up healthy physical balance should not be based on someone else's, just as your destiny dream should not be from someone else; it should be your own. You must determine what is a healthy weight for you. You must determine the frequency and right type of exercises that are best for you. You must determine what the right diet is for you. The key is to make these determinations, with the help of your physician or health professional, and hold yourself accountable to take action to consistently maintain them. No one is perfect, so you will need to make some adjustments to find the right balance. Once you find that balance, create the inspiration and discipline to stay with it if you want to achieve your life plan and destiny.

Financial focus is the understanding that the ongoing acquisition and application of financial knowledge and active management to drive fiscal stability directly affects emotional, physical, mental, and spiritual health. I purposefully use the word *focus* instead of *acumen* because it intimates obtaining knowledge to consistently hold yourself accountable to take action—in this case, consistently building the financial stability and ultimate freedom that will benefit your holistic balance and personal well-being. Without taking the time and attention to effectively focus in this area, it will be difficult to stay convicted and to proactively and prudently maintain healthy financials. Poor personal financial planning, stability, and health invariably will lead to increased stress, resulting in damaging personal, family, and career consequences.

Mental sharpness is the practical application of the knowledge that maintaining, building, and continually improving your mental processing capability directly affects emotional, physical, mental, financial, and spiritual health and capacity. I purposefully use the word *sharpness* because it's analogous to the disciplined process required to maintain a sharp blade or your mental edge. This result can be positive to your well-being if you actively work your mind, like your body, on a regular basis, but it can be negative if you ignore exercising your mind to keep it sharp and informed. The conviction to challenge and stretch your mind and to maintain a healthy continuous learning lifestyle are important factors in improving your holistic balance and personal well-being. Over the course of a typical week, I dedicate ten to fifteen hours to reading, thinking, ideating, and reflecting, with a minimum daily target of one hour per day. Former United States president Barack Obama, Microsoft founder Bill Gates, and many other successful people commit to scheduled reading and thinking time as part of their daily routine. According to CNBC, Berkshire Hathaway founder and legendary investment guru Warren Buffett invests 80 percent of his time into reading and thinking. Furthermore, research carried out by habit and wealth creation expert Tom Corley shows that 85 percent of successful people read two or more self-improvement or educational books per month.

EXERCISE

How would you rate your holistic balance and personal well-being? Estimate where you feel you are right now on the following scale, with zero being the lowest and ten being the highest. Then write at least three reasons that influenced your rating.

 0   1   2   3   4   5   6   7   8   9   10

Reasons:
_____
_____
_____
_____
_____

CHAPTER 18

THE A-ATTITUDES OF LEADERSHIP PERSONAL TRANSFORMATION SELF-ASSESSMENT

To conclude the A-attitudes of leadership development, it is important to reflect on the personal transformation journey that has been initiated. The purpose of this exercise is to recognize your completion of this section and to cement your learning and understanding. Before moving to the next section, take the time to reflect on your A-attitudes of leadership learnings and complete the following personal transformation self-assessment. Be sure to save a copy for your ongoing reference.

1. In your own words, explain the objective of the foundational tier.

_____
_____
_____
_____

   A. Define what authenticity means to you and describe your authentic self.

   _____
   _____
   _____
   _____

B. Define what assuredness means to you and describe your level of self-assuredness.

2. In your own words, explain the objective of the intrapersonal tier.

    A. Define what accountability means to you and describe your current level of holding yourself accountable.

    B. Define what action means to you and describe your current level of taking action.

3. In your own words, explain the objective of the interpersonal tier.

A. What does accessibility mean to you? How would you rate your level of accessibility and how well you leverage it?

B. What does adoration mean to you? How would you rate your level of sharing adoration and how well you leverage it?

4. In your own words, explain the objective of the apex tier.

A. Describe your life philosophy and how it is or can be influenced by the amalgamation of all the tiers.

5. What do holistic balance and personal well-being mean to you?

6. Summarize your key A-attitudes of leadership learnings, including holistic balance and personal well-being, and how you might leverage them to take better control of your life and make your destiny happen.

_____

_____

_____

_____

SECTION 5

MILESTONE 2: THE iLEAD CHANGE MODEL

**Destiny Development Delta Model
The Three Major Milestones
of the Deployment Model
and Key Deliverables**

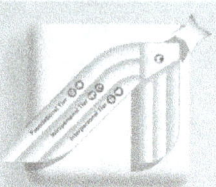

ATTITUDES
OF LEADERSHIP

The A-Attitudes of
Leadership Personal
Transformation Model

Holistic Balance and
Personal Well-being

The A-Attitudes of
Leadership Capability,
Development to Support
Your Transformation

iLEAD
CHANGE

Destiny Development
Delta Life Plan

iLEAD Change
Capability, Processes,
and Models to Activate
Your Life Plan

FORMULA
FOR SUCCESS

The Comprehensive
Destiny Development
Delta Model
Deployment Process

Progress Tracking
and Measurement
Assessment

Dedicated Coaching,
Mentoring, and Support

CHAPTER 19

MAIN MESSAGES OF SECTION 5

In this section, I will describe and explain the following:

- The iLEAD change model in greater detail and the ways it leverages the *how* of your A-attitudes of leadership transformation and development of personal well-being and holistic balance to build and sustainably activate your life plan.
- iLEAD change *inspire*, which is the *i* in the model, and detail the critical importance of its principal objective, which is the construction of the life plan.
- iLEAD change *light*, which is the *L* in the model, and detail its purpose, which is to clearly articulate the life plan to inspire yourself and engage others.
- iLEAD change *engage*, which is the *E* in the model, and detail its goal, which is to build a network of relationships that cultivates the supporters you will need to help you achieve your life plan.
- iLEAD change *activate*, which is the *A* in the model, and detail its prime intent, which is to build process rigor to continuously deliver your commitments to make your life plan a reality.
- iLEAD change *develop*, which is the *D* in the model, and detail its essential aim, which is to indoctrinate it into your Development Delta core mindset of continuous learning to best navigate the dynamic changes and challenges in the road ahead to ensure the success of your life plan.
- Key support models, processes, and personal stories to help bring the iLEAD change model to life.

CHAPTER 20

THE iLEAD CHANGE MODEL

The objective of section 5 is to explain milestone 2 of the deployment process, iLEAD change, in greater detail. The focus is on manifesting your personal transformation in the construction of your life plan and on leveraging the iLEAD change capability and the proprietary support structures, models, and processes to both activate and sustain it.

The *iLEAD* concept represents the *destiny* in the Destiny Development Delta model because it provides the process for setting the future state of your life and legacy. *Change* represents the *development delta* aspect of the model because it provides the never-ending learning, capability building, adaptability, and adjustments needed to successfully navigate the ongoing dynamic turbulence and unforeseen challenges that we face in our lives and in the world every day, to ultimately achieve our life plan and legacy.

Remember that the iLEAD change model is a descriptive acronym representing the words *inspire, light, engage, activate,* and *develop.* It's the *what* of the Destiny Development Delta model that provides a clearly defined road map for you to operationalize your transformation into the action of controlling your destiny. See figure 20.1 for a visual representation of the iLEAD change model.

FIGURE 20.1: THE iLEAD CHANGE MODEL

Milestone 2: The iLEAD Change Model

Milestone 2 begins with the *inspire* section, which is focused on leveraging the deep self-awareness and A-attitudes of leadership transformation developed in milestone 1 to establish your authentic and assured desired future destiny and for you to build the life plan to make it happen. The next section, *light*, is focused on creating the clarity of communication of your life plan to successfully inspire yourself and others and recruit their support. *Engage* is the next section, which increases your capability to build relationships and networks of supporters. The penultimate section is *activate*, which is all about activating your plan and sustaining it over time to achieve your life goals. The final section, *develop*, introduces the concept of the Development Delta core mindset and focuses on continually building new capabilities to enable you to quickly adjust and adapt to both planned and unplanned life, environmental, and social changes to remain on track.

Although the principal objective of milestone 2 is the creation of an authentic and assured life plan, iLEAD change capability building is designed to operationalize your overall leadership to make you the most effective leader you can be. The next five chapters are dedicated to breaking down the five components of the iLEAD change model: inspire, light, engage, activate, and develop. These chapters will include a detailed summary of each iLEAD change component, an introduction of a few proprietary models and processes, and personal stories and examples to vividly bring them to life.

CHAPTER 21

THE iLEAD CHANGE MODEL: INSPIRE

Inspire, as part of the iLEAD change model, is defined as the ability to influence, move, or guide by divine or supernatural inspiration. It is the feeling of awe, wonder, and transcendence that you might experience when you look up and see an eagle soaring high in the sky above the clouds and seemingly touching the sun. It takes our breath away and reminds us that anything is possible when we believe that we can fly like that eagle. Inspiration is also about touching and capturing the hearts and minds of those around us to share that feeling of belief that we can accomplish incredible things together if we commit to making it happen.

FIGURE 21.1: THE iLEAD CHANGE MODEL–INSPIRE

Therefore, inspiration is the most important leadership behavior because it enables us to compel ourselves and others to passionately pursue a grand vision with the determined belief that it can and will be achieved. But inspiration must start with your leadership because you must inspire and lead yourself first to justify and gain the support and help needed to attain your destiny life goals. I will reiterate something that I have previously mentioned several times about leadership: It doesn't matter whether you are viewed as a leader today. What matters is that you begin to see yourself as a leader going forward. You are the leader of your life, and to control your destiny, you must always see yourself as a leader.

According to Marissa Levin in her article "Why Great Leaders (Like Richard Branson) Inspire Instead of Motivate," Branson, the famous entrepreneur, "identifies the ability to inspire as the single most important leadership skill." Additionally, Levin notes a recent Harvard Business

School study that concluded, "The ability to inspire stood out as one of the most important competencies. It is the trait that creates the highest levels of engagement, it is what separates the best leaders from everyone else, and it is what employees want most in their leaders."

Great leadership is about inspiring yourself and others to do something incredible that you and they never thought possible. Inspiration is not focused on gaining followers; rather, it's about inspiring others to see the challenge or opportunity and decide for themselves to passionately commit and hold themselves accountable to act. Orrin Woodward, a *New York Times* best-selling author and *Inc.* magazine Top 20 Leader, says it best: "Average leaders raise the bar on themselves; good leaders raise the bar for others; great leaders inspire others to raise their own bar."

One of the greatest inspirers of people in recent history was Dr. Martin Luther King Jr. He inspired people to put their lives on the line for the cause of civil rights. He changed the United States and the world and was awarded the Nobel Peace Prize mainly because of his unparalleled ability to inspire people. Dr. King was a brilliant and gifted speaker, and his talent and level of global influence can't be matched, but the process he followed can be replicated by you to inspire in your network. He had a dream for the future (equality for African Americans and other marginalized groups and the elimination of poverty) that he deeply believed in; he had a high-level plan to make this dream a reality (nonviolent protest); and he had a very clear, passionate message to articulate the dream in a way that touched and captured hearts and minds. This enabled him to inspire the masses and to recruit passionate supporters who were committed to driving change. This is a perfect example of the iLEAD change model illustrating how inspiration is the catalyst. No one can inspire like Dr. King could, but you can follow the iLEAD change model, on a much smaller scale, to generate inspiration and support for your life plan if you truly believe and are deeply committed to it.

The biggest hurdle is convincing yourself to believe in your vision for the future and that you can control your destiny. Shonda Rhimes, the creator of such incredibly successful television series as *Grey's Anatomy* and *Scandal* is an author and one of the most successful television producers and television and movie writers of this century and was named one of the 100 people who help shape the world by *TIME* magazine in 2007. Here is a quote from Ms. Rhimes regarding deeply believing in your vision: "I remember saying, very almost jokingly, I'm going to take over the world through television, that's my plan. And I said it to my agent, and I said it to my friends, and I said it to myself."

Developing this depth of belief is why the A-attitudes of leadership foundational tier is so critical to inspiration, because possessing the authentic and assured belief in our life plan direction makes it much easier for us to inspire others to believe as well. Serena Williams has said on several occasions, "I always believe I can beat the best, achieve the best. I always see myself in the top position." Do you think Serena's coaches and support network would have had the same belief and passion in supporting her quest to be the best if she didn't believe herself? No, I don't think so.

Tom Brady, who is recognized as one of the greatest football players of all time, won seven Super Bowls over his record twenty-three year career in the National Football League (NFL). That is more Super Bowl wins than any player, or franchise, for that matter. Unbelievably, Brady was not drafted until the sixth round. One hundred ninety-eight players and six quarter backs were selected ahead of him. The message from the NFL was that they saw him as an average player, a back-up quarterback at best. After being drafted by the New England Patriots, he famously told team owner Robert Craft that he (Brady) is the best decision their organization has ever made (Brady has clarified recently that he actually said something like they'd never regret drafting him). Either way, it's clear that Brady believed in himself and was inspired to prove that the NFL was wrong in its assessment of him.

Brady proved that he wasn't average, but he wasn't just good or great either. He was the best, the greatest winner in league history. He began to inspire his teammates to believe that no matter how many points they were behind, or how difficult the circumstances, if they played together as a team and sacrificed for each other, he would always lead them back to victory. He inspired them to believe that they would not only win more games but more championships than anyone. And between 2000 and 2020, the New England Patriots won 164 games and six Super Bowls, the most during this period of any NFL franchise.

It's clear that the ability to inspire, both yourself and others, is the most important aspect of the iLEAD change model. In this chapter, we will illustrate how to inspire yourself first and foremost by developing and manifesting your desired path. You will leverage your personal transformation achieved in the A-attitudes of leadership model to establish your personal source of inspiration and your desired future destiny and to build your life plan to achieve that destiny. You will develop the capability to assess and pressure test your desired future destiny and life plan to ensure that they truly represent what you authentically want and whether you assuredly believe and are fully committed to them. Building your life plan in this way crystallizes your personal source of inspiration and will allow you to inspire others.

Over the next several pages, you will find personal stories and examples to vividly bring *inspire* to life for you. These stories and examples will be followed by the introduction and description of the Destiny Development Delta life plan model.

INSPIRING THE TEAM TO RAISE ITS OWN BAR

As I referenced earlier, I was promoted to manager for the first time in 1995 while working for a large US-based food manufacturing company, just a little more than two years removed from college. This was unexpected and happened only because the union employees, unbeknownst to me, started a petition to influence management. At the time, this factory was one of the largest food manufacturing facilities in the world and produced half of the company's production volume, making it strategically important and material. But the plant's performance had been steadily eroding, productivity was down, and financial targets had not been achieved in five straight years. In addition, the culture was fraught with poor management and labor relations, resulting in excessive union grievance filings. Something had to change and fast.

My first course of action was to connect with everyone in the plant to understand what they felt the issues were, how they were being affected, and what they thought we should do. I met with everyone individually, including our salary management and support staff, union leadership, and team members, across the three shifts. I also spent significant time on each shift on the production floor with operators and technicians as they did their jobs, asking for their thoughts on what could be improved. I then had shift team meetings and town halls to make sure there was inclusiveness and transparency. I told the team that I would review all the feedback and develop a skeletal improvement plan to bring back to them for their input and that we would agree on a final plan together that everyone could buy into. But before I could get back to them with the draft plan, things started improving dramatically and incredibly fast.

Within two months after I became the manager, our production line performance increased by 25 percent, our ingredient waste reduced by a third, and, incredibly, we had our first two months of favorable financial performance in five years. The culture was also changing, as evidenced by a 50 percent reduction in union grievances. It was hard to understand what was driving this from my standpoint because I hadn't presented a draft of the improvement plan, much less aligned a finalized version.

I went to one of my mentors who had been at the plant for twenty-five years. I said to him, "Ganesh, I don't understand what's happening. We're making big improvements fast, but I haven't really done anything. I haven't finalized a plan or implemented any changes yet. What's going on?"

Ganesh replied, "I've been here twenty-five years and have never seen this kind of turnaround. So yes, it is incredible. But you are not correct that you haven't done anything yet. Never underestimate the power of people liking you. You showed genuine care to the people; that's why they pushed for you to be the manager. Then you immediately showed they were right about you by meeting with each one of them, spending time with them on the shop floor, and requesting their input. They're inspired to ensure that you're successful. They're determined to not let you fail." The people were inspired to raise their own bar.

INSPIRING DRAMATIC PERSONAL TRANSFORMATION

Here is a great example of inspiration driving personal transformation for an individual who was a big part of the turnaround I just referenced. This personal story is very important to me and was a critical moment in my development and understanding of the influence I could have on people through inspiration. It created a realization that informs my thinking even today, because I experienced the power of inspiration on transformation firsthand and have seen it and lived it many times since.

When I became a manager for the first time as referenced in the prior story, I knew all of my new direct reports well because I had been part of the team as a peer for a year and a half. However, after I was promoted, I took the time to meet with each one of them to clarify expectations, for both me and them, based on my new role. I also wanted to understand what their personal drive was, what was in it for them, what their key talents were that maybe I wasn't aware of, and what they were most passionate about. Once I understood this, I would reorganize the team to better match the individuals with roles that they had both passion for and the talent to do well.

The second-shift packaging operations supervisor was a cantankerous middle-aged guy named Mitch. During our one-to-one meeting, I said, "I think you're a really good packaging supervisor. Is that what you really want to do?"

He answered, "I don't think it matters much, but although I like what I do, my dream was always to be in maintenance. But I know I'll never get that chance because I don't have a technical degree, and I don't have the support of management."

I immediately remembered when I worked second shift with Mitch that I saw firsthand that he had excellent technical troubleshooting skills and a great relationship with the packaging mechanics. I replied, "Mitch, I think you'd be great in packaging maintenance, and I will fight to make it happen if that's what you really want."

He said, "OK, but I won't hold my breath because the senior management will never agree to it."

The next week, after securing approval for my recommended organization changes, of which Mitch's transfer to maintenance was one, I met with Mitch to give him the good news. He was stunned, and from that day forward, Mitch's entire demeanor changed from irritable and gruff to positive and excited. Mitch became one of my top performers and biggest supporters throughout my time there.

After I decided to leave the company a few years later to pursue another opportunity, the team had a going-away party for me. The celebration was fantastic, and a really good time was had by all. Everyone came up to me and said their heartfelt goodbyes and expressed sincere well-wishes. When the festivities started to die down, I finished my final beer, made a toast to the team, and bid them good night. Mitch asked if I would go outside with him before I left while he smoked a cigarette. For as long as I live, I will never forget what happened next.

Once outside, Mitch, this rough and tough guy, started crying. Then he looked up and said, "Before you leave, I have to tell you something. It's hard to say, but here goes. I've been a racist my entire life. I hated Black people and never wanted anything to do with them. And then I met you. Of all the bosses I have ever had, you're the only one who ever believed in me enough to give me a chance to achieve my dream. All my other bosses were white, and I asked them all for a chance in maintenance, and all of them shut me down. But the one person who I didn't want as my boss because of his skin color proved to me that I was wrong by not prejudging me and by giving me a chance. I just wanted you to know that I was committed to not let you fail because you changed my life forever, and for that I am forever grateful."

As defined earlier, *inspire* is the ability to influence, move, or guide by divine or supernatural inspiration. But also, inspiration, as brought to life in Mitch's story, is about touching and capturing hearts and minds and about influencing people to deeply feel and believe in something, even if it is counterintuitive to their existing core beliefs, and being willing to take accountable action to transform themselves to support it, protect it, and ensure its success. Mitch's story and Bill's from section 2 are two of the most important for you to remember from this book because they clearly and vividly illustrate the incredible power of inspiration to transform.

INSPIRE CAPABILITY DEVELOPMENT AND THE BUILDING AND ACTIVATION OF MY LIFE PLAN

The intent of relaying the previous stories is to illustrate how the power of inspiration touches and captures hearts and minds and moves people to do things they did not think were possible. Bill's and Mitch's stories are perfect examples, as each man thought they were beyond the ability to change, much less transform.

Inspire leverages your A-attitudes of leadership capability to transform and crystallize your authentic goals and assured commitment to build and activate your life plan. As I relayed earlier, I constructed my life plan when I was twenty-four years old. I developed it to be the road map for my journey to take control of my life and make my destiny happen.

Prior to constructing my life plan, I was unconsciously stuck in the cycle of no destiny control. I was doing a lot of good things and taking positive actions, but I lacked strategic and deliberate directional focus. I was the hamster on the flywheel. But then, as I mentioned in section 2, I had a big breakthrough that initiated my escape from the cycle when I connected with my authentic self and made the difficult decision to quit college football in my senior season. After taking a semester off, I made the assured decision to return to university to pursue a Master of Science degree. But I had not yet held myself accountable to authentically decide what I wanted to do long term. I had not yet answered these questions: What future destiny do I want for myself, and what do I want my legacy to be?

FIGURE 21.2: DONZEL IN THE CYCLE OF NO DESTINY CONTROL

The birth of my son was the seminal moment that pushed me to fully transform and break out of the cycle of no destiny control. It was the moment I understood that I could no longer be a chameleon, making incremental changes and adjustments while holding on to the safety blanket of knowing that I could always go back to the way it was, the way I was. I had come to the realization that it was time for me to be the caterpillar and to authentically and assuredly commit to what I wanted my destiny and legacy to be. I needed to enter my chrysalis, transform myself, and emerge anew, as my own unique butterfly.

I started this transformation process by doing the hard work of establishing the authentic and deep understanding of what I truly wanted. I forced myself to envision where I wanted my life to be at sixty-five years old. I envisioned what our family would look like and what our well-being would be. I envisioned what I wanted my career to have been, what I would have accomplished, and what I wanted to be doing with my career postretirement. I envisioned the societal influence I would want to have made and how I would increase that influence going forward. In summary, I envisioned the legacy and destiny I wanted, and I was truly inspired by it. I shared my destiny vision with my partner and best friend, my future wife, Tracy, to test whether she was inspired by it, ensure that she was aligned to it, and that there was integration with what she wanted for herself and her destiny and with our family.

I then used my authentic and inspired destiny vision to develop my first life plan and establish the road map to activate it. I knew that I could not make my destiny happen alone and that I needed help and support beyond Tracy. I realized that I had been extremely fortunate in my life to have received support from many people to help me get to where I was. Clearly, continuing to grow my network and gain more inspired supporters to help activate my life plan and achieve my destiny was critically important. But equally important to me was making a significant positive influence on as many lives as possible by modeling the A-attitudes of leadership capabilities and inspiring people to raise their own bar. I wanted to bring others along with me as I moved forward and inspire them to achieve things that they did not think were possible for themselves.

Many of the stories included in this book profile people who, in some way, influenced or affected my life trajectory by either actively engaging to help me or providing me the opportunity to help and support them while developing and leveraging my A-attitudes of leadership capabilities through reciprocal inspiration.

I have been continuously activating my life plan ever since its construction and have successfully achieved my goals and objectives with regard to family, community, career, financial stability, and, most importantly, holistic balance and personal well-being. I have continued to be inspired by my personal brand to strive to be the best to make my destiny happen, and it is gratifying to be living the plan that I envisioned more than thirty years ago. But as I stated, my ability to inspire myself to build, activate, and live my plan would not have been as meaningful if I had not also developed and leveraged my ability to inspire others to engage and support me.

Inspire, as part of the iLEAD change model, combines developing your ability to inspire yourself and others with achieving the deliverable of facilitating the building of your personal life plan. This combination is akin to the old saying "killing two birds with one stone" because you're furthering your transformation by learning and building capability in the critical skill of reciprocal inspiration while fully leveraging your authenticity and assuredness to discover and unleash your own personal source of inspiration—your desired future destiny with a life plan to achieve it.

Here are the perspectives of two of my mentees, Michael and Elena, regarding *inspire*:

Michael:

> Having a defined life plan this early in my life is great. It's a perfect time for me at this early stage and provides advantage for me going forward. I recently graduated from college, I was planning to get engaged to my longtime girlfriend, I was also starting my career with my very first real job. I now have the long-term clarity that many of us in our early twenties don't have. I have a plan to work from that includes goals for my personal and professional life and that focuses on my overall long-term destiny and well-being. And it is great to know that as things change, which they will because I am so young and the world always throws things at you, I have a game plan for my life that I can call audibles from or modify when I need to. It also allows me to have more clear conversations with my fiancée about our future together. Overall, having a life plan that I developed and feel good about allows me to better manage stress and uncertainty and provides great peace of mind.

Elena:

> Although I have always been family focused, there was a time when I allowed my career to take precedence over my family and I got out of balance. My personal well-being suffered, and I had to take a step back. Since then, I have not spent a lot of time thinking about what my career ambition could be because I didn't think it would fit with my family focus. Donzel coached me through holistic life planning, which forced me to really think deeply about what I am capable of doing and what I want to do long term and how to do it in a way that maintains my personal well-being and holistic balance. On top of that, I benefited from Donzel's coaching and belief and investment in me personally and professionally. I have grown because I have been fortunate to have him walking along the path with me. My focus on my long-term plan and continued coaching and support will propel my career and family fulfillment.

BUILDING THE DESTINY DEVELOPMENT DELTA LIFE PLAN

Inspire is about developing an authentic and assured vision, stepping up to lead, and motivating yourself and others to make it happen. As part of the Destiny Development Delta model, *inspire* also has the principal deliverable of guiding you through the building of your life plan. The Destiny Development Delta life plan model is a step-by-step approach that will lead you to identify your dream or vision of the future, assess what it will take to get there, and build your life plan to make it a reality. It is comprised of five distinct steps: (1) envision destiny, (2) current state, (3) gap analysis, (4) milestone plan, and (5) activation plan. Figure 21.3 provides a visual of the model, followed by an overview of each step.

FIGURE 21.3: DESTINY DEVELOPMENT DELTA LIFE PLAN MODEL

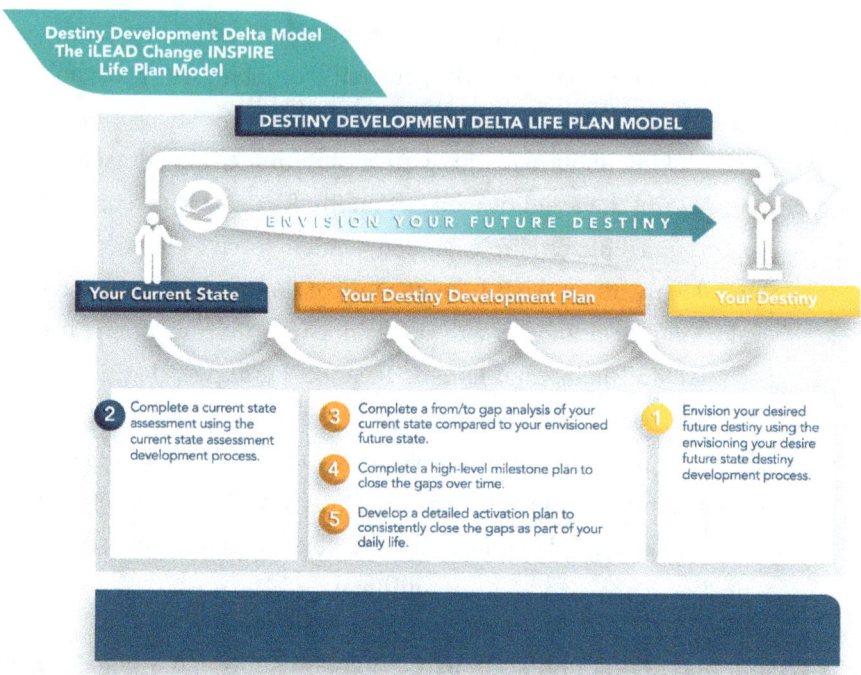

Step 1: Envision Your Destiny

The first step in developing your life plan is to envision your desired destiny. This involves establishing your authentic dream and vision of the future by following our envision your destiny process.

Here is the perspective of one of my mentees, Delphine, regarding envisioning her future:

> It has not been easy for me to think about or plan out my future. It is difficult for me to think about the future and what I can do differently from today and ongoing to shape it. I have never really had a career plan in mind. I just went to college to be an engineer, then took the best job. From there I took new jobs based on the opportunity that was presented. No strategy at all,

just taking what came up that sounded interesting. I was like the dandelion seed, allowing chance to dictate my career. Donzel coached me to truly envision my future. He asked me where I wanted to be in fifteen, twenty, twenty-five years. I had not ever thought about this and really didn't know how or where to start. But he coached me through this, and I realized that at thirty-eight, it would have been nice to have done this ten years prior, but it was still a very good time for me to start this important work for myself. Donzel helped me see that it wasn't too late. I now have a long-term plan that represents what I want and aligns with my family as well. I am more personally fulfilled and more driven professionally, and I feel that it will only get better now that I have a plan.

Figure 21.4 presents this process, followed by a description.

FIGURE 21.4: ENVISION YOUR DESTINY PROCESS

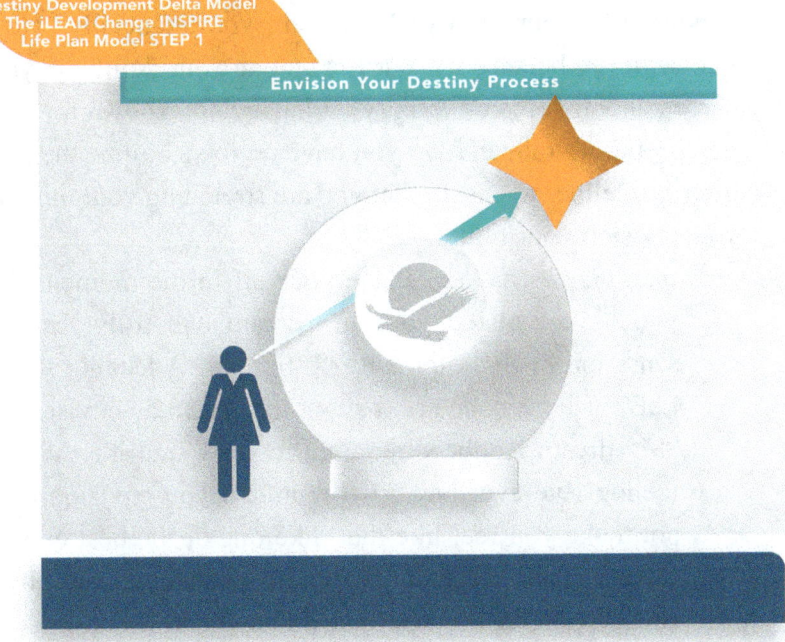

Imagine yourself at a later stage of your life, select a target age (i.e., forty, fifty, sixty, or seventy) when you feel you would be old enough to reflect back and determine whether you are achieving or have achieved what you wanted in life. In other words, look through the *inspire* crystal ball that functions like the Mirror of Erised, the magic mirror in J. K. Rowling's world-famous book series Harry Potter, of which Hogwarts Headmaster Albus Dumbledore said "shows us nothing more or less than the deepest, most desperate desire of our hearts," and ask it to reveal your desired destiny. Here are the recommended steps to help you on this magical journey:

1. Decide on a target age and envision your destiny track or the legacy you want to have established. This is not the destiny that someone else wants for you, and, quite possibly, it's not the one you thought you wanted or are currently on track for. This must be the destiny that you truly desire deep down, authentically and assuredly. Here are a few questions to consider: How do you feel about this destiny and legacy? What are your most important accomplishments? What is the condition of your family? Where are you financially? Have you achieved balance in your life among your family, in your career, and in your community? What are you known for? Are you proud of yourself? Do you have regrets? Follow the next three guidelines to ensure that you are stretching your mind as you envision your future.
    a. *Imagine the feeling.* Place yourself in the moment that you have realized your life dream and truly feel the sensation of that moment. All-time NBA leading scorer LeBron James once said about the dream he envisioned, "My dream has become a reality now, and it's the best feeling I've ever had." If the dream you envision does not make you feel like that, like one of the best experiences of your life, then you are not pushing yourself hard enough to envision what you authentically want.

b. *Know that it is never too late.* Drake, one of the world's best-selling musical artists, said, "It's never too late to realize what you want in your life and it's never wrong to fight for it." You have to believe that no matter where you are in life right now, the authentic dream you envision is still within your reach if you hold yourself accountable to build and activate your plan urgently and relentlessly, as if your life depended on it. LeBron James, who achieved another of his improbable dreams in 2024 by becoming the first father to play with his son on the same NBA team in his twenty-first season, also said about dreams, "Dream as if you'll live forever, live as if you'll die today."

c. *Think big.* Nelson Mandela once said, "There is no passion to be found playing small—in settling for a life that is less than the one you are capable of living." This is your life. Make it worth living. As you envision your dream, no matter what it is, don't settle. The late Brazilian national treasure Pelé said, "If you are first, you are first. If you are second, you are nothing." Jack Ma, the cofounder of Alibaba, said, "If Alibaba cannot become a Microsoft or Wal-Mart, I will regret it for the rest of my life." Vincente Guerrero is a national hero in Mexico who dreamed big and made those dreams a reality by emerging from humble beginnings to be one of the leading generals in the triumphant revolutionary war over Spain. He would later become Mexico's second president and the first Black president of an independent nation in the Americas.

2. Force yourself to do an honest reality check to ensure that your future destiny vision is truly authentic and representative of what you really want. Ask yourself: Does it align with my A-attitudes of leadership development? Is it representative of my A-attitudes life brand? Does it pass "The Person in

the Glass" test? How do I think it will affect my holistic balance and personal well-being? Do I assuredly believe in and commit to achieving it, and what would I sacrifice to make it happen?

Step 2: Complete a Current State Assessment

The second step in the Destiny Development Delta life plan process is to complete a current state assessment to gain a clear understanding of where you are today. This begins with a personal development assessment and then integrates a SWOT analysis to identify your strengths (areas in which you excel), weaknesses (areas in which you struggle), opportunities (areas that you've underleveraged or underdeveloped and/or where changes in circumstances could benefit you), and threats (areas that will derail you if you don't improve and/or adjust to changes in circumstances).

For an effective current state assessment, you must be honest and transparent with yourself about your current life situation. Think of it as a detailed person in the glass assessment, where your image in the glass has experienced Gringotts Wizarding Bank's Thief's Downfall, from J. K. Rowling's Harry Potter book series. This is the magic spell that washes away all other spells, disguises, incantations, and concealments to reveal the actual person as they truly are. The current state assessment process, as seen in figure 21.5, requires that you view yourself clearly from three different perspectives. The first two come from referring back to your A-attitudes of leadership the person in the glass reflection and personal brand development and transformation assessment, and the third comes from completing a candid and thorough SWOT analysis.

FIGURE 21.5: CURRENT STATE ASSESSMENT PROCESS MODEL

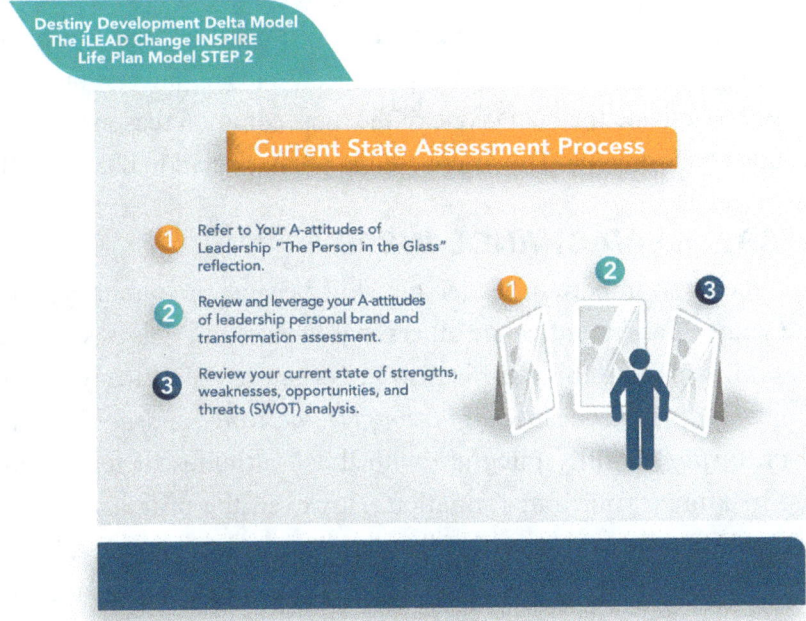

Step 3: Complete a from/to Gap Analysis

The third step in the Destiny Development Delta life plan process is to complete a from/to gap analysis. This entails developing a clear understanding of what you must do and what needs to happen in the future to achieve your destiny. This is done by conducting a future state SWOT analysis and then completing a from/to gap analysis compared to your current state to thoroughly understand the differences and to develop a high-level gap closure plan.

Step 4: Create a High-Level Milestone Plan

The fourth step is to create a high-level milestone plan to close the gaps over time to achieve your destiny. This involves leveraging the gap analysis from step 3 to establish major milestones that must be accomplished to achieve your future state envisioned destiny goal.

Step 5: Develop a Detailed Activation Plan

The fifth step is to create a detailed activation plan to progressively close the gaps as part of your daily, weekly, and monthly routine to consistently deliver the major milestones and ensure that you achieve your life plan. This is key to making your destiny happen because losing interest or drive to consistently activate the plan is one of the most common reasons people don't achieve their dreams. This is covered in greater detail in chapter 24.

SUMMARY: iLEAD CHANGE *INSPIRE*

Inspire is the most important leadership skill because it enables you to motivate yourself and to influence others to join your cause as passionate supporters. Developing this skill is also important to the efficacy of the iLEAD change model because *light*, *engage*, *activate*, and *develop* all depend on *inspire* to fully integrate with the A-attitudes of leadership model to maximize your transformation. However, the principal objective of iLEAD change *inspire* is to build your Destiny Development Delta life plan, and in so doing, crystallize your personal source of inspiration.

The Destiny Development Delta life plan process is a methodical, step-by-step approach that will lead you to identify your dream or vision for the future and build your life plan with clear and measurable milestones, support processes, and structures to make it a reality. From a high-level strategic perspective, it helps you identify your desired destiny, understand the gaps you must close to get there, and develop an actionable plan to make your destiny happen. The process is comprised of five distinct steps:

1. Envision your destiny.
2. Complete a current state assessment.
3. Perform a from/to gap analysis of your current state compared to your envisioned future state.
4. Create a high-level milestone plan to close the gaps over time.
5. Develop a detailed activation plan to progressively work to achieve your milestones as part of your daily life.

CHAPTER 22

THE iLEAD CHANGE MODEL: LIGHT

ight, as part of the iLEAD change model, is defined as the ability to illuminate and stimulate sight to make the way forward visible and clear. It requires vision of a desired outcome or goal, why it is worth pursuing, and a strategic or high-level plan that illustrates how it can be achieved, even if on the surface it appears impossible. As Helen Keller once said, "The only thing worse than being blind is having sight but no vision." Light is most powerful when there is a vision, or true North Star goal, that not only benefits that person but also creates positive game-changing impact for other people, the community, and/or the world. A good example is Dr. Martin Luther King Jr.'s dream for a better United States of America and world in general. As Dr. King stated during his acceptance speech in receiving the 1964 Nobel Peace Prize in Oslo, Norway, "I have the audacity to believe that peoples everywhere can have three meals a day for their bodies, education and culture for their minds, and dignity, equality, and freedom for their spirits . . . I still believe that one day mankind will bow before the altars of God and be crowned triumphant over war and bloodshed, and nonviolent redemptive good will proclaim the rule of the land . . . I still believe that we shall overcome!"

FIGURE 22.1: THE iLEAD CHANGE MODEL–LIGHT

A clear vision with a high-level plan that shows that something is possible, coupled with inspiration and engagement for a mutually beneficial outcome, can drive breakthrough performance and success by empowering and enabling people to accomplish things they did not think possible. Viola Davis is the first Black actress to earn the so-called triple crown of acting, winning an Academy Award, a Tony Award, and an Emmy Award. In both 2012 and 2017, Ms. Davis was named by *TIME* magazine as one of the world's 100 most influential people. She had to overcome many obstacles to become regarded as one of the best actresses in the world, and she had to have authentic inspiration, assured belief, and a clear vision of her goals to persevere. According to Davis, as quoted in *Essence* magazine in August 2011, "As Black women, we're always given these seemingly devastating experiences—experiences that could absolutely break us. But what the caterpillar calls the end of the world, the master calls the butterfly. What we do as Black women is take the worst situations and create from that point."

To control your own destiny, you must be able to light the way to your desired future vision. Yet most people spend only a fraction of their time truly pondering their future to develop a clear personal vision. Over the course of my career, I have spent more than fifty thousand hours in one-on-one meetings with greater than ten thousand people from all over the world, and I can tell you from personal experience that fewer than 10 percent were able to tell me what they wanted to accomplish in their lives, what their long-term career ambition was, or even simply where they wanted to be in five years. Here are a few additional data points. A Harris poll showed that nearly 50 percent of working adults and job seekers have either a rudimentary career plan that is not well thought out or no plan at all. The same study also found that fewer than 60 percent of working professionals believe they are living up to their career potential, and only 5 percent have met with their human resources teams to discuss their career trajectory. Clearly, this is not controlling your destiny. To do that, you must have the authentic self-insight to develop a thoughtful and assured vision that truly inspires you to make it happen and that you can articulate confidently to others so that they choose to help you.

In this section, the focus is on teaching you how to light the way to making your life plan a reality by leveraging your development in the A-attitudes of leadership model and the iLEAD change *inspire*. *Light* means being able to craft and tell your story in a way that is both inspiring and authentic to you and your audience. This is important as you prepare to move to iLEAD change *engage*, where you will heavily leverage your clarity of vision and ability to communicate to diverse networks and audiences in ways that each of them can understand and identify with personally. Shonda Rhimes, one of the greatest producers and writers of film and television of this century, said in relation to understanding the medium of your audience, "Writing for television is completely different from movie scriptwriting. A movie is all about the director's vision, but television is a writer's medium." As you develop your capability to light, you will learn how to make it your medium for communicating in a passionate, illustrative, and confident way so that people can feel, picture, and ultimately be inspired by what you've envisioned.

Over the next few pages, you will find a personal story and an example to vividly bring iLEAD change *light* to life, followed by the introduction and generalized description of one of our proprietary development processes.

BLAZE THE TRAIL

Here is an excellent example of how *light*, in support of *inspire*, can be leveraged to make great things happen, including transforming moribund organizations into record-setting standard-bearers. Several years ago, following a major acquisition at my company, I was promoted from the established heritage business to lead operations in the newly acquired company. These operations encompassed eleven facilities spread across three countries. I was unfamiliar with them, so I spent a significant amount of time traveling to each facility to understand the technology, identify the opportunities, and, more importantly, get to know the people and the cultures. I quickly discovered that we had passionate leaders and awesome people, but, unfortunately, these locations had experienced underinvestment in both capital and human capacity and thus had been left behind after being acquired, as most of the company's focus, attention, and resources had been on the established heritage businesses. It also became clear that because these locations had been deprioritized and effectively forgotten, it left the team feeling like they were second class.

However, it was obvious to me that their potential had been grossly underestimated. In fact, I theorized that if we had a unified vision and an improvement plan and if I could get the team to believe and work together, we could not only make dramatic performance improvements but also outperform the established heritage operations. This was almost blasphemous to ponder because the heritage operations had set the performance standard in our company and were recognized throughout our industry. Additionally, it was generally accepted across both organizations that because of the differences in technology, regulatory requirements, and perceived people capability between the heritage and the newly acquired operations that it was impossible for us to outperform them.

I knew that due to the business realities at the time, it would not be prudent to immediately infuse these operations with incremental investments and resources, so there needed to be another solution. The answer came to me during one of our subsequent leadership team meetings. I had just said that I was convinced we had the talent and the passion not only to significantly improve our performance to the point that we would quickly become the best in the company but also to set new company standards that would rival world class if we all committed to make it happen. Then I saw the look in their eyes—their authentic pride because I had basically said that I believed in them and had faith that we could be the best in the world. I had inspired them to think that maybe they could accomplish something that the company and they themselves had never thought possible. Now I had to convince them that we could do it by magnifying that inspiration with a crystallized message identifying a simple but logical plan that detailed how we would pull it off if we all committed. I had to light the way.

The next day I met with my leadership team again and asked if they thought we could be the best performers in the company and if they were willing to commit to pursuing this goal. They all agreed. I then said, "That's great, but I believe we can do better than that." I asked them, "Would you be willing to embark on a trailblazing journey to transform our operations to being among the best in the world?" Before they could answer, I told them that I was convinced we could do it because I believed in them and because I had a clear, logical, and simple three-step plan to make it happen. I relayed my experience from benchmarking many facilities worldwide and pointed out that the very few that were performing at a world-class level were following this same basic plan. I also said that I knew from personal experience that our established heritage operations were not doing these things because although these three steps are easy to understand, they are hard to do and even more difficult to sustain, requiring continuous process rigor and high-level leadership commitment and engagement. I then detailed the three-part strategy.

I said, "First and foremost, we must inspire our people with a simple rallying cry to excite and unite everyone behind the goal." I suggested Blaze the Trail because we set out to do what no one else had done, and we would create the path for everyone else to follow. We would build excitement and pride in our teams and inspire them not only to go from worst to first but also, like Captain Kirk from *Star Trek* would say, to "boldly go where no one has gone before." We also knew that we had to be a united team because it was going to be a difficult and arduous journey, and as the old African proverb says, "If you want to go fast go alone, but if you want to go far go together." This was an important cultural dynamic to foster and avoid the established heritage operations' long history of purposely not working closely together due to a rewards system that heavily incentivized them to compete against one another.

Second, we would fully engage all team members in the Blaze the Trail objective regardless of their role on the team. We would do this by ensuring that it was reflected in each team member's personal objectives and by providing a structured time for everyone to work on performance improvement together as a team, focusing the strength of our resources on the biggest opportunities.

Third, we would adopt a methodical and rigorous continuous improvement work process as our standard operational practice. Everyone agreed, and we set the aggressive goal for our Blaze the Trail objective to achieve world-class performance in three years or less, which was one-third the average time required for other operations that had reached this performance tier.

The impact was fast and dramatic, even though the activation of the continuous improvement process was not smooth and had to be adjusted several times, as initially it was too complex and laborious. But the inspiration of blazing the trail to world class and lighting the way to making it happen with a simple and logical three-step plan was so powerful that it overcame this problem. This is a classic example of how great buy-in with an average strategy almost always beats a great strategy with average buy-in.

During the two years we were blazing the trail, the results were astounding! Our team's performance increased by greater than 50 percent, we delivered almost a half a billion dollars in productivity, and we tripled our overall output capacity. But what I was most proud of was the confidence and pride that was now pervasive across our operations. The team no longer viewed themselves as laggards but as leaders and trailblazers who had the assured belief that they were among the best in the world. I had established a vision that I deeply believed in and that I was able to inspire my team to believe in as well. I then articulated a high-level plan illustrating how we could do it if we all worked together. Finally, I convinced them that we would accomplish what even they initially thought was impossible. This is the combined power of *inspire* and *light*.

THE MESSAGING MAGIC PROCESS

Light, as part of the iLEAD change model, is defined as the ability to illuminate and stimulate sight to make the way forward visible and clear. It requires both a vision of a desired outcome and a strategic or high-level plan that illustrates how it is possible to achieve, even if it appears impossible. One of the things that separates the Destiny Development Delta model is dual development, meaning that as you build your capability in each focus area for everyday application, you are also doing what's necessary to move your life plan forward. This is true in *inspire*, where we develop your capability to motivate and energize while also building your life plan, and in *light*, where we develop your strategic communication skills while lighting the way for you to engage others and activate your plan. We do this by leveraging the messaging magic process. Over the next few pages, I will explain the process and provide a visual model for illustration.

The messaging magic process is designed not only to develop your messaging capability but also the specific deliverable of illustrative communication to inspire people. Picturing for others your vision through your words is especially important to engage supporters to help activate your life plan. Here is what one of my mentees, Michael, said about this:

> Using messaging magic was really key in helping me simplify what I want to do long term into a succinct message. This is important to me as I start my career and life to be able to communicate clearly to positively and confidently represent and advocate for myself to be prepared to take advantage of opportunities no matter when and where they are presented.

What is messaging magic? It's the art of developing clear and inspirational messaging and consistently delivering it with such skill, effectiveness, and confidence that it feels like magic.

Messaging is defined by dictionary.com as "a system or process of transmitting messages, especially electronically, by computer, telephone, television, cable, etc., or a communication containing some information, news, advice, request, or the like, sent by messenger, telephone, email, or other means, and as an official communication, as from a chief executive to a legislative body." The common link between these three definitions is sending or presenting information to others, but what's most relevant to us is the concept in the final definition that it is a formal communication from an authority. This is critical because the key for you to understand is that every time you send a message, you are communicating as the authority, the leader, the CEO of your life, and what and how you communicate paints the picture of yourself to others.

Magic is defined by dictionary.com as "the art of producing illusions as entertainment by the use of sleight of hand, deceptive devices, etc., or the art of producing a desired effect or result through the use of incantation or various other techniques that presumably assure human control of supernatural agencies or the forces of nature." The common link between these two definitions is the word *art*, which is a skill that can be developed. This is critical because many people think that it is only through deception or the forces of nature that certain people have the ability to communicate both clearly and inspirationally. But if you have an authentic and assured belief in something, like your life plan, you can nurture and develop the art of powerful, clear, and inspirational communication.

The messaging magic process focuses first on understanding and defining the *what, to whom,* and *why* and then on developing the best communication that lights the way to facilitating inspiration and engagement. The *to whom* and *why* questions are most critical because, more times than not, the deciding factor of the influence and effect of your communications is not based on what you said but rather on who you said it to and how it was delivered. The objective is to create inspiring messaging that touches both minds and hearts by speaking directly to each listener in language that feels like their own, highlighting specifically what's in it for them, to successfully engage them to become part of your network of passionate supporters. Nelson Mandela said, "If you talk to a man in a language he understands, that goes to his head. If you talk to him in his language, that goes to his heart."

The messaging magic process poses the following three questions, then presents a process to facilitate comprehensive responses to provide the base ingredients to build the communications to most effectively light the way:

1. What is your objective?
2. Who is the audience?
3. What is in it for them?

Once these three questions have been considered and responded to comprehensively, the remainder of the process is leveraged. Figure 22.2 shows the messaging magic process for generating clear and inspirational communications.

FIGURE 22.2: DESTINY DEVELOPMENT DELTA MESSAGING MAGIC PROCESS

SUMMARY: iLEAD CHANGE *LIGHT*

Light, as part of the iLEAD change model, is defined as the ability to illuminate and stimulate sight to make the way forward visible and clear. It requires vision of the desired outcome, why it is worth pursuing, and a strategic or high-level plan that illustrates how it is possible to achieve. It is important to understand that every message you send paints a picture of who you are and what you are about. Developing confident and purposeful communication skills while also facilitating the activation of your life plan is done by leveraging the messaging magic process.

Messaging magic focuses first on defining what, to whom, and why you are communicating and then provides a process to craft your story so that your audience can easily understand it. This is important preparation for the next chapter, as we move to iLEAD change *engage*, which focuses on recruiting passionate supporters to help you activate your life plan.

CHAPTER 23

THE iLEAD CHANGE MODEL: ENGAGE

*E*ngage, as part of the iLEAD change model, is defined as the ability to attract, bring together, or interlock people to commit to or take part in something. Engagement is powerful because it functions like a voluntary contract to work together to jointly drive and own mutually beneficial outcomes as a committed interdependency over an extended period of time. Engagement differs greatly from involvement, which implies optional interaction with no formal commitment to outcomes. This is why couples don't formally announce when they first become involved. Couples do formally announce when they become engaged because it's a serious commitment. It's similar in effect to what Dr. Martin Luther King Jr. said about the commitment or engagement with nonviolence: "Nonviolence is absolute commitment to the way of love. Love is not emotional bash; it is not empty sentimentalism. It is the active outpouring of one's whole being into the being of another."

FIGURE 23.1: THE iLEAD CHANGE MODEL-ENGAGE

To maximize the power of engagement, one must personally commit to engaging others and empowering them to be full partners in making a transformative vision a reality. Then United States senator Barack Obama understood this clearly when he delivered the keynote address at the 2004 Democratic National Convention: "There is not a liberal America and a conservative America—there is the United States of America. There is not a black America and a white America and Latino America and Asian America—there's the United States of America." This was the first time that he'd spoken on a national stage, and it was key in enabling him to engage an unprecedented diverse coalition of support that resulted in his historic election in 2008 as the first Black president of the United States and to maintain that engagement to win reelection by landslide standards in 2012.

In the *inspire* chapter, we learned how to create a life plan based on your dream destiny, but no dream worth achieving can be accomplished without the help of at least one other person and, even more likely, a very large network of supporters. Jack Ma, who cofounded Alibaba and is the former executive chairman of Alibaba Group, said, "My dream was to set up my own e-commerce company. In 1999, I gathered eighteen people in my apartment and spoke to them for two hours about my vision. Everyone put their money on the table, and that got us $60,000 to start Alibaba." *Engage* is about securing and sustaining commitment, like Jack Ma's eighteen supporters, by capturing hearts, minds, and then hands and by driving transparency, inclusion, relationship building, communication, and alignment through consistent, sincere, and effective interpersonal investment.

As I stated earlier, all successful people have had help from others along the way, and some of the most important assistance came from unexpected places. The key is to inspire and engage by first capturing hearts and then by touching minds. Abraham Lincoln, whose election sparked the country's only civil war, recruited for his cabinet highly qualified individuals, all of whom were his rivals at the time. According to Doris Kearns Goodwin, author of *Team of Rivals: The Political Genius of Abraham Lincoln*, Lincoln explained, "In order to win a man to your cause, you must first reach his heart, the great high road to his reason."

The best leaders focus on character and freedom to operate, which are key ingredients to creating an environment of all-in engagement, where everyone feels empowered and committed to a common objective. According to the HOW Report, leaders who focused their time and effort on shaping character across an organization were rated by 96 percent of their workforce as effective leaders, and their organizations were more than three times as likely to deliver exceptional performance. However, this type of engagement is rare, as a recent Gallup survey found that fewer than 35 percent of employed people report feeling engaged, committed, and enthusiastic with their work. Anyone who can create true engagement and sustain it will have a multiplicative competitive advantage, whether in business or in their personal life.

Engagement, coupled with inspiration and a clear vision and plan to light the way for a mutually beneficial outcome, can drive breakthrough performance and success by empowering and enabling people to accomplish things they did not think possible. United States Representative for New York's fourteenth congressional district Alexandria Ocasio-Cortez, known by her initials AOC, is a perfect example of how *engage* coupled with *inspire* and *light* can accomplish the seemingly impossible. In the June 2018 democratic primary, she accomplished the unthinkable and defeated the ten-term incumbent democratic caucus chair, Joe Crowley, even though she was only twenty-eight years old, virtually unknown, and had so little campaign money that, according to her, she at times ran her campaign out of a paper bag. It was considered the biggest political upset of the 2018 campaign year. She was able to pull off this incredible feat by engaging and inspiring people who had been ignored for years with a clear vision and message of hope and action. According to AOC, "People try to identify who is the most likely person to turn out, and what we did is that we changed who turns out. And that changes the whole electorate . . . The only time we create any kind of substantive change is when we reach out to a disaffected electorate and inspire and motivate them to vote."

NFL legend Tom Brady not only left a legacy as the greatest quarterback of all time, but also one of the best teammates. His ability to unite and influence a diverse group of people, inspiring them to work together relentlessly to achieve the common goal of winning, was unparalleled. Opponents disliked playing against him, but his teammates cherished him, not only because they believed he could lead them to championships, but also because of the respect he showed them. Even though he was one of the most famous athletes in America, Brady sometimes wore his name on his helmet during training camp like the new players, and occasionally, he would stay after practice to help them learn the offense. When the New England Patriots acquired Antonio Brown, a player with a controversial past, Brady opened his home to Brown to show everyone that he welcomed Antonio with open arms. Tom Brady's emphasis on accessibility and adoration fostered genuine engagement and was crucial to his success in leading two franchises to a total of seven Super Bowl victories.

It is understandable to think that not everyone can inspire and engage like the people I cited in previous examples, but you can develop this capability with strong focus and coaching in the A-attitudes of leadership and the iLEAD change models.

Here is a personal story to bring *engage* to life and to illustrate the power it creates, followed by the introduction and general description of two of our proprietary development processes and models.

ADVERSARIES TO PASSIONATE SUPPORTERS

Early in my career, I accepted a position with a large multinational company to be the production manager at one of their biggest US manufacturing plants. The factory employed more than five hundred mostly long-tenured union members who produced greater than a third of the company's volume. The plant's management and union leadership had a long history of difficult labor relations.

The production department was the largest in the plant and employed several of the most tenured team members. Two of the most influential were Tammi and Brett, a married couple with decades of seniority and an extensive relationship network throughout the plant. They were well connected, respected, and liked by their peers. They also had a very close personal friendship with the former production manager, Chip, whom I had replaced. Brett, Tammi, and Chip had worked together in the plant as union employees many years ago but maintained a friendship, even after Chip's promotion to management.

Within a month, I realized that Tammi and Brett were going to be a problem for me. First, as I mentioned, I was hired to replace Chip. In their mind, I was the young hotshot brought in to replace their close friend. This was not my fault, but my arrival meant Chip's exit, and they made it clear that they were not happy I was there. Second, I discovered that Tammi had been receiving preferential treatment from Chip regarding overtime scheduling. This allowed Tammi, who had fewer years in the plant than Chip and most of the people on first shift, to choose whatever overtime she wanted to work and to decline what she didn't, resulting in others being forced to work both weekday and weekend overtime in her place. This also meant that Tammi could never be drafted or forced to work overtime. Many employees were upset about this arrangement, and who could blame them; it violated the union contract and simply wasn't fair. But because Chip and Tammi were so well connected in the plant, no one, not even the union leaders, wanted to address it.

Another reason many team members wouldn't formally complain was that Brett was a technical genius and a great teammate. He knew the processing systems better than our engineers and liked to help other operators and mechanics solve their technical problems. He had enough seniority to work day shift but chose to work nights in part to help inexperienced junior operators, many times skipping his breaks to do so. Even though many peers were frustrated that Brett's wife was getting preferential treatment, no one would formally challenge it in fear that he might stop helping them. But people did complain to me off the record, and it was a growing source of festering unrest in the department. As the new leader, I knew that at some point I had to address it and sooner rather than later.

Sooner came faster than I expected, as the scheduler alerted me that we did not have enough volunteers to work the weekend and that we would have to draft or force some employees to work. The scheduler said that Tammi's name was first on the list to be drafted and then asked whether I was exempting her as the prior manager had. I told her that there was no reason that I was aware of that would exempt Tammi from being drafted to work if her name was next on the seniority list per the union contract.

Tammi was placed on the weekend schedule, and when she and Brett found out, they angrily came into the office to confront me. Tammi said forcefully, "You had no right to take me off the exempt list." When I asked why, she responded, "Because we had a deal with Chip that we'd be exempt if I helped babysit his kids." I told them I was sorry but that was preferential treatment that violated the union contract and the rights of more than five hundred other people. They got even more agitated, and Tammi demanded, "So you're not changing it?" I asked if she had a reason that would qualify for an exemption, and she responded that she had plans that weekend.

I replied, "Tammi, again, I am very sorry, but there are five hundred people in the plant who have plans this weekend, and, unfortunately, you're one of the twenty who have to change their plans because, according to the contract, it's your turn to work."

Brett said, "I'm not helping anybody in this plant anymore. And you'll be really sorry then, because performance will be in the tank. And don't ever try to talk to me." Before they left the office, Tammi threatened, "We're going to make you pay for this!"

I knew I had done the right thing by taking a stand and stopping the favoritism, but obviously there were going to be consequences. As the saying goes, no good deed goes unpunished, and I knew Tammi and Brett were real power brokers who could easily disrupt my ability to lead the organization effectively. The next week Tammi announced that she was running for union steward and let me know that her reason was to make my life as the new manager as difficult as possible.

I had work to do to somehow salvage this situation and decided to start by placing additional focus on my relationship with Tammi and Brett with the intent of at least moving them from negative to neutral. I was confident that Tammi would win the union election, requiring me to meet with her regularly and providing many opportunities to build a better relationship. It wouldn't be easy, but the opportunities would be there. I decided to focus on Brett first, since he worked third shift and I saw him less frequently. I usually arrived at five thirty every morning to walk the shop floor and connect with everyone on night shift before they went home at seven, but I started coming in at four thirty to have an extra hour to connect with Brett.

The first week that I arrived early, I headed to Brett's area. As soon as he saw me, he would leave the area and disappear before I could get there to speak with him. The second week he stayed there and sat in the control room. I would go in, greet him, and talk directly to him, but he would look straight ahead and not acknowledge me at all. By the third week, I think he realized I was not going to stop coming in, so he started to talk but only about problems in the plant, like machine defects and maintenance needs. This was great because I would listen intently and list every problem he brought up that night to follow up on during the day and build credibility with him.

During the sixth week, he ran out of problems to complain about because they had all been fixed, so we finally started having real conversations. We talked transparently about what had happened. He told me that he understood why I stopped the special treatment and apologized for the confrontation. I said that I should have handled the situation with more care by talking to him and Tammi first. From there we started to build a positive relationship. I shared my vision for the organization and asked for his feedback and input. He felt honored that I asked and provided great perspective. We both looked forward to our early-morning talks about life, family, and sports and our shared vision of how to make the plant better. After a while, he started helping everyone on third shift again. But Brett didn't stop there. He started coming in early and staying late to help people on the other shifts as well, and this influenced others to do more. It wasn't long before we not only gained back the performance losses we had sustained but also improved significantly beyond that to levels we hadn't reached historically.

Not surprisingly, Tammi won the election. True to her word, she was a very tough and difficult union steward. But the more we worked together, the more she saw that I was a high-character guy just trying to do the right thing, and the more I saw that she was a strong and fair leader who only wanted the best for her people. We also realized that we had a lot in common. We both were dedicated parents and most of our spare time was spent supporting our kids. Eventually, we discussed the incident, and she apologized for yelling and threatening me and said that after becoming a steward, she understood why I had to stop the favoritism. I told her how much I respected her courage and leadership and how I believed that she and I together could make a big difference in the plant.

From there we started to build a very positive relationship. Tammi and I worked together as collaborative partners, not as union and management representatives, to improve work rules and conditions for the benefit of our entire organization. During the time we worked together, workplace injuries and union grievances were cut in half.

A little over a year after the confrontation, it was clear to me that Tammi and Brett were no longer negative adversaries, but I didn't realize just how much things had changed until two major events occurred in my life.

In July 1998, I was playing catch with a football with my then five-year-old son in the backyard. I called to him to throw me the football, and he did. I threw it back to him and told him to run and score a touchdown before I tackled him. He laughed and started running away from me. I chased him, and when I caught up to him, I tried to reach around him to knock the ball out of his hand. At that moment, my right foot stepped on the heel of his left foot, and he fell down. When he tried to get up but couldn't, I looked at his leg. My heart sank because I could tell that his femur was broken.

We rushed him to the hospital thinking he just needed to have his leg set in a cast and then we could go home. But we soon realized that this was much more serious than we'd thought. The doctor told us he had a spiral fracture and that based on the location of the break, he would have to be in traction in the hospital for three to four weeks. My wife and I were stunned and shaken, and of course I felt terrible. I called work and told them what happened and that I would be staying at the hospital with my son for the next four weeks. A few days later, he received his first visitors: Tammi and Brett. They brought him some coloring books and candy and told me not blame myself for what had happened. They said that I was just being a good dad playing with my son and that an accident happened. Then they told my son how much everyone loved me at work and that I was one of their best friends and they would do anything to help my family and me. Tammi and Brett touched my heart and uplifted me at one of the lowest points of my life. Their visit cheered up my son, but it meant the world to me.

A year and a half later, I accepted a transfer to the corporate office. I had reservations about leaving after fewer than three years at the plant, but I knew it was best for my family. During my going-away celebration, I received many cool gifts and testimonials, including being one of the very few in management to ever be given a union jacket, which I still have today. But the most gratifying and moving gift came from Tammi and Brett. They gave me a gold star paperweight that was impressive in and of itself. But it was the engraving that made it so very special. It read: "Donzel Leggett, A Leader of Star Quality." It brings tears to my eyes to think about it even now. I have set that star in the most visible and prominent place in every office I've had ever since to remind me of Tammi and Brett and how the power of engagement can transform adversaries into passionate supporters and, more importantly, dear friends.

ENGAGE PROCESSES AND MODELS

As stated at the outset of this chapter, *engage* is the ability to bring together people to commit to accomplish something great together. It's powerful enough to turn adversaries into passionate supporters by capturing hearts and minds through consistent and sustained A-attitudes of leadership relationship building. Anyone who wants to achieve something great, something that leaves a positive and indelible legacy, must engage other people for help. I had developed a clear and strong life plan to accomplish my desired destiny, but I knew I wouldn't be successful if I didn't engage others to build a network of inspired and passionate supporters to help me. Barack Obama spoke about this during a speech in Roanoke, Virginia, during his 2012 reelection campaign: "If you've been successful, you didn't get there on your own . . . I'm always struck by people who think, Well, it must be because I was just so smart.' There are a lot of smart people out there. 'It must be because I worked harder than everybody else.' Let me tell you something—there are a whole bunch of hardworking people out there. If you were successful, somebody along the line gave you some help."

Here is the perspective of Anita, one of my mentees, regarding *engage*:

> The idea of building a network of supporters is something that I knew was important. I stayed in contact with mentors who helped recruit me into the company and had been my managers. I also stayed connected with some of the people I worked with. I built strong connections with several of my sorority sisters after graduating from college. I thought my network was pretty good. In working with Donzel, I learned that for the career and life objectives that I had in mind, my network was actually pretty narrow because it was focused only on people who were already naturally in my network, people I had lots of interests in common with, and work peers and people perceived as senior mentors. In other words, it was not a very diverse network. Donzel shared his engagement models and processes with me and coached me to implement them to build a much more expansive and diverse network with deeper connections. As a result of this, my support group increased fivefold, and many of my life goals that had stagnated began to come to fruition in short order. Not just career goals but, more importantly for me, personal life goals that dramatically affected my well-being in a super positive way. With my ever-growing network of diverse supporters, my future is bright.

Over the next few pages, I will introduce and explain two of our *engage* models that illustrate how to begin building a network of inspired and passionate supporters.

PERSONAL INFLUENCE INVERTED PYRAMID MODEL

One of the most important concepts to understand about *engage* is that for it to have strategic impact, it must be managed strategically. The personal influence inverted pyramid provides structure to assist you in strategically managing your engagements by prioritizing your time and maximizing your effectiveness across important but distinct groups. It segments different forms of communications to various constituencies into four distinct layers based on factors such as access, type and closeness of relationship, and objective of your message. Each layer represents a constituency and suggests a total time allocation and frequency of communication based on their strategic importance in helping activate your life plan. The first layer, one-to-one interpersonal connections, is by far the most critical of the four because it's the most assured way to establish the deep connections and relationships necessary to recruit and build a strong and expansive network of inspired and passionate supporters.

FIGURE 23.2: DESTINY DEVELOPMENT DELTA PERSONAL INFLUENCE COMMUNICATION INVERTED PYRAMID

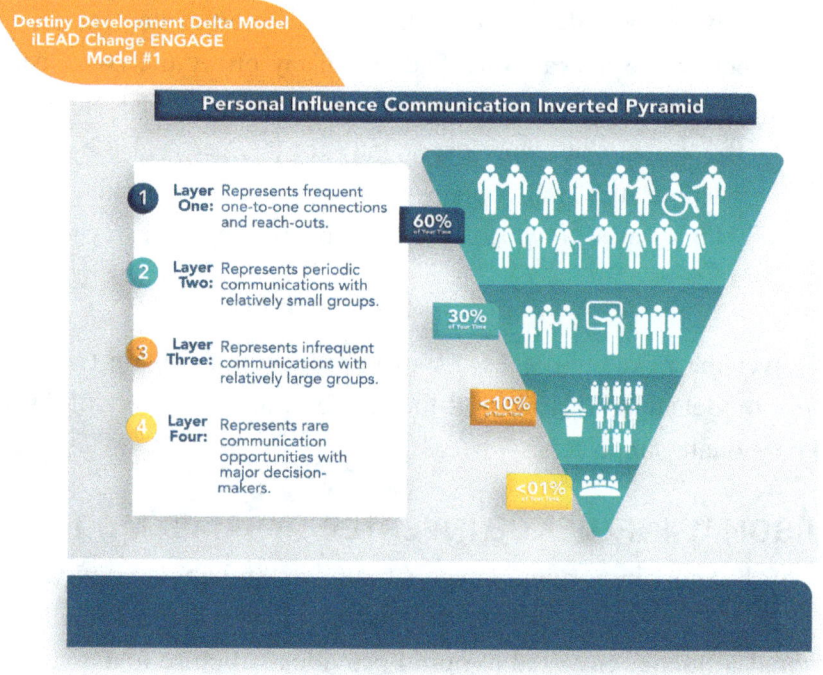

SAWUBONA-IFY "I FEEL YOU" MODEL FOR ACCELERATING RELATIONSHIP BUILDING

The personal inverted pyramid provides structure and prioritization to build an expansive network while the Sawubona-IFY "I Feel You" model offers the capability development process for accelerated relationship building. Sawubona-IFY helps crystallize the A-attitudes of leadership capabilities into a targeted approach to best ensure that the investments you are making in time, effort, and diligence of relationship building pay off. This model is intended to assist in accelerating relationship building by helping create trust, respect, and a deeper connection with assured accessibility and authentic adoration. The Sawubona-IFY model will not only help you accelerate and deepen relationships quickly but also proactively sense and address potential points of conflict and misalignment, underscoring your strengthening connection.

FIGURE 23.3: THE SAWUBONA-IFY "I FEEL YOU" MODEL

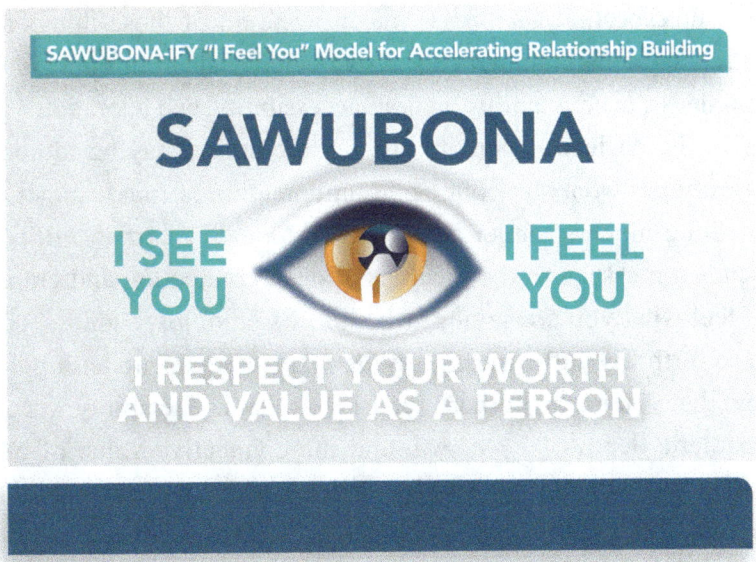

The Zulu tribe is the largest ethnic group in South Africa. King Shaka united many different tribes to form the Zulu empire in 1818. They were the last indigenous empire in South Africa, prior to British colonial rule being enforced after the 1878 Anglo-Zulu War. Today, the Zulu people number between ten to twelve million, which represents about 23 percent of the South African population. Zulu is also the most common language spoken in South Africa. With the Zulu people having both a long and rich history in South Africa and the fact that they are the majority ethnic group, it stands to reason that there would be some aspects of their culture that would permeate the rest of the country. One such cultural practice is *Sawubona*, which is the most common greeting in the Zulu tribe. *Sawubona* means "I see you, just as you are, I know you are here, you are a valuable person, and all my attention is on you." This is a much greater and connective meaning than the Western greetings of *hi, hello,* or *what's up* and even *how are you doing*, as most people say these phrases out of habit and expect a similarly superficial response back. On the rare occasion when someone does reply with their actual feelings, especially if they aren't good, the greeter is caught off guard and doesn't know how to respond. This is because in many Western cultures, greetings are more about courteousness than genuine care, feeling, and respect. *Sawubona* is meant to be all of those things and more to drive immediate mutual connective value enabled through authenticity, assuredness, accountability, action, accessibility, and adoration.

In the African American culture, a common saying to convey that you truly get what someone is communicating is *I feel you.* It connotes something much stronger than *I understand* or *I know what you mean.* It sends a message to the receiver of deep connection and empathy that you feel what you are saying, whether it's pain, joy, sadness, confusion, and so forth. By authentically saying *I feel you,* you are letting the person know that you are right there focused on them. The ability to convey the empathetic depth of *I feel you* and the connective value of *Sawubona* enabled through the A-attitudes of leadership model creates a powerful capability that will significantly accelerate relationship building to inspired and passionate support.

Additionally, we now interact electronically through virtual meetings, texting, social media, and other electronic platforms more than in person, but having the majority of your interactions through technology, although more efficient, can make it increasingly difficult to establish deep interpersonal connections. However, even in this environment, you can still build strong relationships by continuously improving your capability of quickly and authentically connecting with people through the Sawubona-IFY model for accelerating relationship building. Whether connecting virtually or face-to-face, the inverted pyramid and Sawubona-IFY models will help you successfully and expeditiously develop a strong and growing network of inspired and passionate supporters.

SUMMARY: iLEAD CHANGE *ENGAGE*

Engage, as part of the iLEAD change model, is defined as the ability to attract, bring together, or interlock people to commit to do or accomplish something substantial. To maximize the power of engagement, you must personally commit to engage and empower others to become full partners in your vision and plan. This chapter focused on introducing and explaining *engage* and illustrating how to leverage it to build a network of inspired and passionate supporters, which you will need to help make your life plan a realty.

In this chapter, we introduced two of our *engage* models. The personal influence inverted pyramid provides structure to assist you in strategically managing your engagements by prioritizing your time and maximizing your effectiveness across important but distinct groups. The Sawubona-IFY "I Feel You" model crystallizes the A-attitudes of leadership capabilities into a targeted approach to accelerate relationship building.

Engage, coupled with *inspire* and *light*, captures hearts and minds to build a network of inspired and passionate supporters whose hands you will need to help you activate your life plan and make your destiny happen. This is important preparation for the next chapter, as we move to iLEAD change *activate*, where we will introduce the structured approach to activate your life plan.

CHAPTER 24

THE iLEAD CHANGE MODEL: ACTIVATE

Activate, as part of the iLEAD change model, is defined as the process of developing and activating, or bringing to life, the detailed plan to achieve your vision and goals to control your destiny. *Activate* predominantly leverages the skills that were built in the A-attitudes of leadership intrapersonal tier of accountability and action because it is about setting goals and targets, making plans to achieve them, and holding yourself accountable to steadily move forward.

FIGURE 24.1: THE iLEAD CHANGE MODEL–ACTIVATE

Benjamin Franklin once said, "If you fail to plan, you are planning to fail." I live my life by this maxim, as I have a plan for everything, and I plan to win. But it is important to understand what I mean by a plan. A plan is a set of strategies and tactics that together, if activated, lay the path to victory. Sun Tzu, the legendary philosopher and military general in ancient China, is recognized as being one of the most ingenious strategists and tacticians in recorded history. He is broadly recognized as the author of *The Art of War*, a book written thousands of years ago that is still regarded as one of the best volumes ever penned on strategy and tactics, with relevance ranging from military to sports to business. I have been reading and referring back to Sun Tzu and *The Art of War* since I was in my early twenties, and two of his most pointed quotes about planning are that "strategy without tactics is the slowest route to victory. Tactics without strategy is the noise before defeat" and that "victorious warriors win first and then go to war, while defeated warriors go to war first and then seek to win." My thought process, influenced by both Ben Franklin and Sun Tzu, has been that I will not plan to fail by failing to plan. In fact, I will plan to win by defining and committing to my authentic goal of winning; developing strategies that I am confident will earn the victory; and clearly identifying, sequencing, and delivering the tactics to achieve each strategy, which will in essence ensure that I win. This is iLEAD change *activate*.

As I mentioned earlier, I have objectives and plans for everything that I do, and those plans have strategies and tactics designed to optimize my chances of successfully accomplishing whatever I am doing. These plans vary in depth and sophistication based on the situation and circumstance, but my activation never varies. In my experience, the 80/20 rule applies to most people's adoption of consistently leveraging plans to reliably achieve their objectives and improve their personal effectiveness and efficiency. In other words, only 20 percent of people rigorously and consistently plan, organize, and place heavy focus on activation, and they are 80 percent more efficient than those who don't. The effectiveness of planning is magnified by being specific about setting timelines and targets and holding yourself accountable. A 2015 study by psychologist Gail Matthews showed that when people wrote down their goals, they were 33 percent more successful. In my experience, this is because the simple act of writing down the goal is a message to our subconscious that we have committed to ourselves that we will accomplish something on a definite timeline, creating the feeling of self-accountability to activate.

Therefore, having a clear vision and a strong committed plan is essential, but what's most important is having the authenticity and assuredness to hold yourself accountable to personally activate your plan. Sachin Tendulkar was listed as one of the TIME 100 most influential people in the world in 2010. Here is what Sachin said with relevance to *activate*: "If you don't execute on your plans, then you don't reach anywhere."

Activating the strategies and tactics of your plan will not be perfect, and you will hit roadblocks, but if you continue to channel your authentic and assured self to inspire, light, and engage, you will find a way keep on track. This is the essence of the much-repeated statement that execution eats strategy for lunch, but in my case I prefer *activation* because it infers bringing life to my plan while *execution* could subconsciously be taken as killing or terminating it, and words do matter.

The bottom line is that having a good plan means nothing unless you activate it. This concept is so important that it is worth repeating: The best vision or desired destiny and life plan in the world will never come to fruition unless you activate it. Shonda Rhimes said this: "I think a lot of people dream. And while they are busy dreaming, the really happy people, the really successful people, the really interesting, engaged, powerful people, are busy doing."

The following is the introduction to and description of the activate perpetual cycle, followed by a personal story and an example to bring it to life.

THE ACTIVATE PERPETUAL CYCLE

As stated at the outset of this chapter, activate, as part of the iLEAD change model, is defined as the process of developing and activating the detailed plan to achieve your desired destiny. Having the self-accountability to activate your detailed plan and the resiliency and determination to stay with it is critical because it will be hard work. You must stay inspired by your life plan destiny because activating it will be tedious and arduous at times and will feel like you are pushing uphill and making no progress. Alibaba cofounder Jack Ma, who was rejected by Harvard Business School all ten times he applied, said, "Most of the important things in the world have been accomplished by people who have kept on trying when there seemed to be no hope at all."

There will be tough times, and you may want to quit, so you will have to decide how badly you want it. How hard and for how long are you willing to work for your destiny? LeBron James said, "Greatness is defined by how much you want to put into what you do." LeBron was ultra talented growing up, and everyone who saw him play knew that he had a rare gift for basketball. His high school games were standing room only events, broadcast nationally on ESPN and attended by NBA legends like Shaquille O'Neal, but there have been other players over the years with über talent similar to LeBron's. Only one is known as the King, and that is LeBron, so what was different about him that allowed him to develop his talent to lead two different franchises to a combined eight straight NBA Finals and three different franchises to NBA Finals Championships, win four NBA regular season and Finals MVP awards, and be the only player in history selected to thirteen All-NBA First Teams? He had a dream to become the greatest basketball player of all time; a plan to get there; and the resiliency, commitment, and determination to work harder than anyone else to make it happen. As LeBron himself said, "Hard work beats talent when talent fails to work hard."

If you want to accomplish something great, it's not enough to have a dream, a plan, and supporters, no matter how authentic, assured, and passionate, if you don't hold yourself accountable to activate and make it happen. You will need to leverage the A-attitudes of leadership model, as well as the iLEAD change *inspire*, *light*, and *engage* concepts, so that they all converge not only to activate your plan but also to convert activation to a source of energy itself. This process is called the activate perpetual cycle.

The activate perpetual cycle provides structure to assist you in strategically, tactically, and relentlessly managing your activation. Remember that *activate* is the process of developing and bringing to life the detailed plan to achieve your desired destiny. According to *Merriam-Webster*, *perpetual* is defined as "going on and on without any interruptions, having an existence or validity that does not change or diminish or lasting forever," and *cycle* means "a series of events or actions that repeat themselves regularly and in the same order." Thus, the activate perpetual cycle is about developing and activating your detailed life plan on an ongoing basis without interruption in a continuous and ordered cycle.

Figure 24.2 is a visual of the overall activate perpetual cycle. At the center is the life plan because the objective of the cycle is to ensure that your life plan is activated and that you continuously and rigorously drive it forward to achieve your desired destiny. It is the tool that facilitates determination to always grind or put in the work to ensure that every day you are earning the right to claim your destiny. The life plan is orbited by the three processes and models that comprise the activate perpetual cycle—the laser focus model, the strategic time management model, and the gamification process.

FIGURE 24.2: DESTINY DEVELOPMENT DELTA ACTIVATE PERPETUAL CYCLE

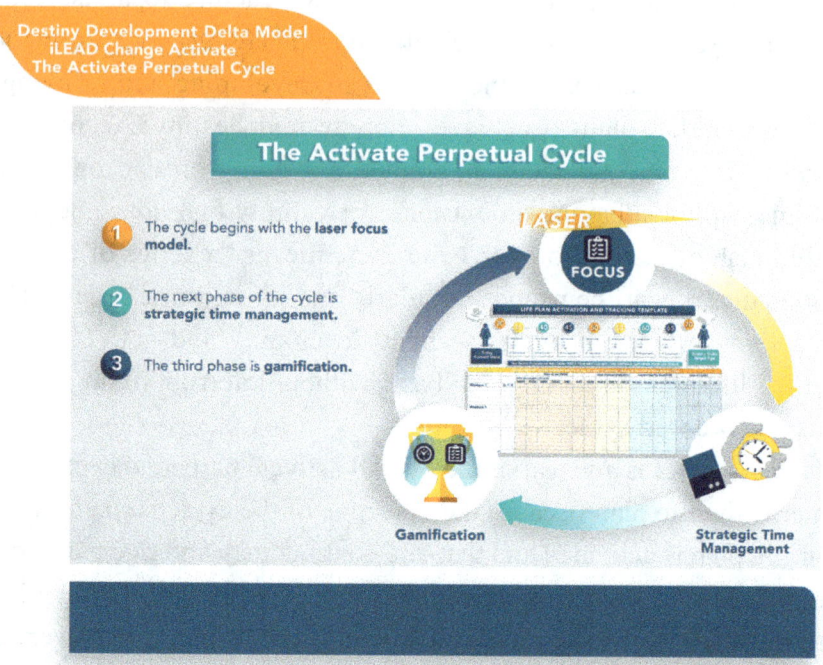

THE LASER FOCUS MODEL

Phase one of the activate perpetual cycle is the laser focus model, which provides the process rigor and routine building to initiate the life plan. We use the words *laser focus* in combination to mean an intense and accurate continuous stream of energy concentrated intently on each strategy and tactical point of your life plan in a deliberate cadence to comprehensively, resolutely, and indomitably activate it. Your life plan is your ticket to controlling your destiny, but it must be activated to take you to your destination. You are accountable for your destiny and thus for your life plan activation. You must be laser focused to cut through all the noise and distractions and not allow for any excuses.

FIGURE 24.3: THE LASER FOCUS MODEL

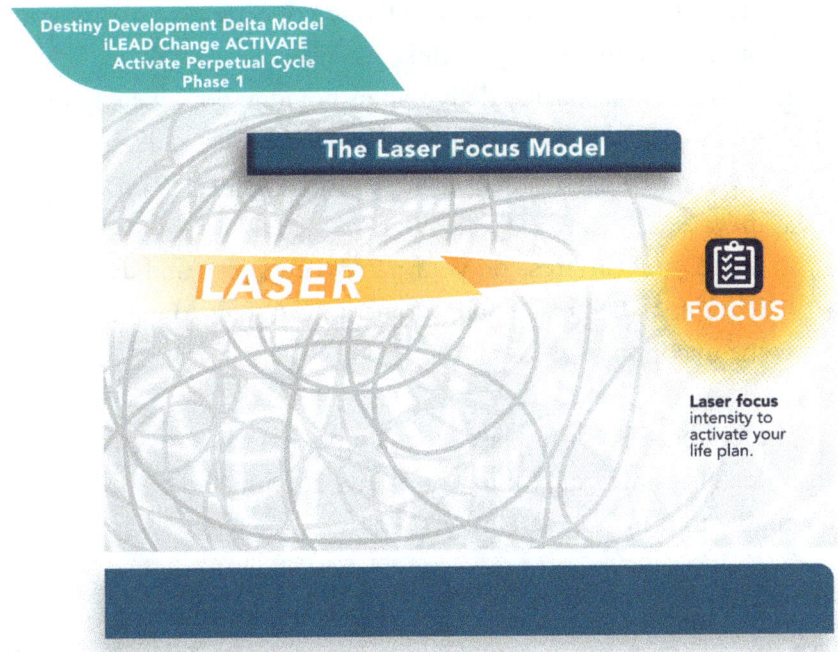

Serena Williams said about focus, "If you can keep playing tennis when somebody is shooting a gun down the street, that's concentration."[1] Serena had a dream to be the greatest tennis player ever, and she and her father had a plan to reach that dream. But Serena, and only Serena, could activate that plan with the incredible passion, commitment, perseverance, and laser focus that would be required to achieve her dream. The laser focus model provides the routine, repeatable cadence that, coupled with the internal strength developed in the A-attitudes of leadership capabilities, will keep you moving forward regardless of disruptions. This model lists the simple steps to build the discipline needed to stay centered and to avoid or work through distractions by creating and following a robust and repeatable routine that continues your march to activate your plan to make your destiny happen.

---

1   Fearless Motivation, "The Greatest Serena Williams Quotes."

Key Steps of the Laser Focus Model

1. Begin by reviewing your detailed activation plan. This provides the key milestones to activate your life plan by integrating them into your daily life.
2. Schedule the specific deliverables noted in your weekly plan.
3. Review your accomplishment of the planned deliverables at the end of each day and make adjustments to stay on track for the week.
4. Score your progress on your past week's plan and debrief for learnings, then make appropriate adjustments to your plan for the upcoming week.

The bottom line of the laser focus model is to have a detailed plan with milestones integrated into your daily routine and to hold yourself accountable to prioritize activation.

THE STRATEGIC TIME MANAGEMENT MODEL

Phase two of the activate perpetual cycle is the strategic time management model, which provides the time allocation planning and discipline to support the laser focus model. Here we use the words *strategic time management* to mean actively managing your time as a measurable but finite resource to accomplish the necessary and important strategies and milestones to fully and successfully activate your life plan. The laser focus model integrates your life plan milestones into your daily routine while the strategic time management model ensures that you accommodate them into your schedule.

FIGURE 24.4: THE STRATEGIC TIME MANAGEMENT MODEL

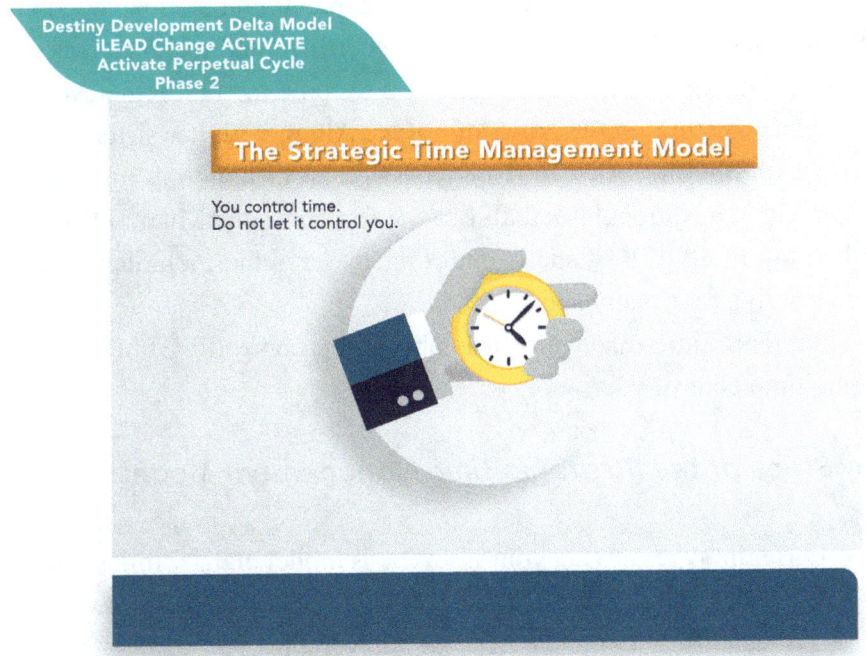

I have referenced Serena Williams multiple times in this book, and she is profiled as part of the activate virtuous cycle more than anyone else. This is because she embodies relentless activation with an intense laser focus on being the absolute best in the world while strategically managing her time to fully activate the other parts of her life plan. Serena knows that it is not smart to wait for good things to just happen for you. Instead, you have to make them happen for yourself by developing a plan and then passionately activating it by focusing and leveraging your most precious resource—time. She knows that you must behave as if there is no such thing as luck. Serena once said in reference to her accomplishments, "Luck has nothing to do with it, because I have spent many, many hours, countless hours, on the court working for my one moment in time, not knowing when it would come."[2] As referenced earlier, Serena wanted

---

2   Fearless Motivation, "The Greatest Serena Williams Quotes."

to be more than a tennis player, and as part of her plan, she strategically managed her time to be holistically fulfilled. While becoming the greatest female athlete of all time, she has also become a mother, developed and launched her own fashion line, become a certified nail technician as part of launching her own nail collection, and become the first female athlete to have her picture on the cover of *Vogue*. Along with her sister, Venus, she became the first African American woman to hold any meaningful ownership in a National Football League franchise, the Miami Dolphins, and on top of all of this, she is multilingual, an author, a philanthropist, and an activist for many social issues.

Strategic time management is about you controlling time and not letting time control you.

Key Steps of the Strategic Time Management Model

1. Begin by reviewing your laser focus model plan by milestone.
2. Assess the amount of time you will need on a daily basis to successfully complete life plan deliverables.
3. Calculate the amount of discretionary time available for each day of the week.
4. Develop a balanced schedule across each day and the full week to ensure that you have adequate time to accomplish your life plan deliverables and to maintain personal well-being.
5. Review and score your compliance to your past week's schedule and debrief for any learnings, then make appropriate adjustments to your schedule for the upcoming week and the rest of the month if appropriate.

The bottom line of the strategic time management model is to actively manage your time as a measurable but finite resource to successfully activate your life plan with laser focus while maintaining holistic balance and personal well-being.

THE GAMIFICATION PROCESS

Phase three of the activate perpetual cycle is the gamification process, which supplements intrinsic motivation by leveraging self-competition and extrinsic rewards. We use the word *gamification* to mean providing incremental fuel, incentive, and motivation to maintain laser focus and disciplined strategic time management to continually activate and accomplish the milestones of your life plan over multiple years and decades.

FIGURE 24.5: THE GAMIFICATION PROCESS

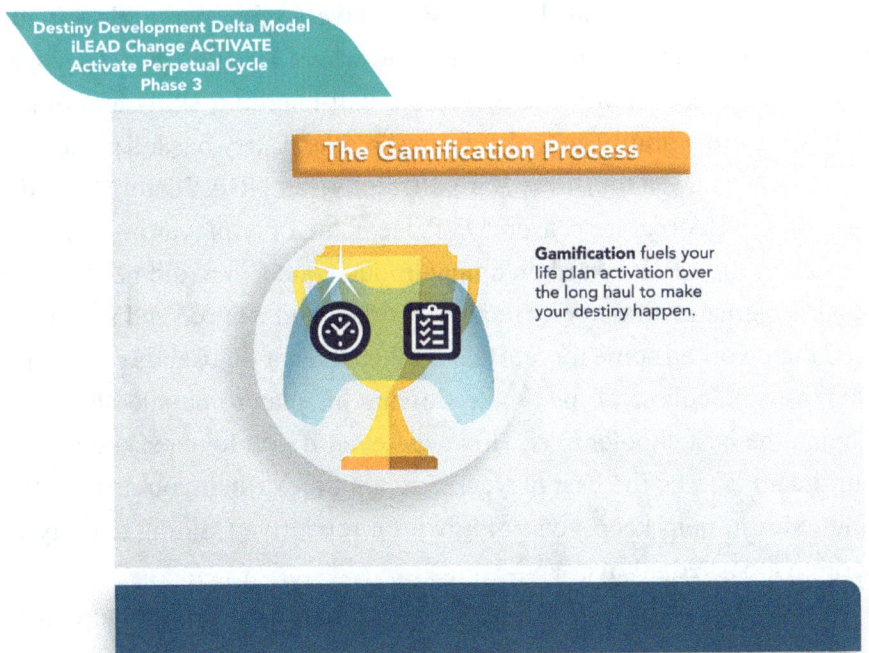

As you activate your plan, there will inevitably be roadblocks and feelings of impending defeat, monotony, boredom, and seemingly never-ending milestones, tasks, and desires to put things off and even quit that you will have to overcome to sustain the active perpetual cycle.

Taylor Swift said, "Fearless is getting back up and fighting for what you want over and over again . . . even though every time you've tried before you've lost." Gamification is about providing extrinsic motivation when you need additional fuel, a turbocharge, or a jolt of energy to keep fighting for what you want and moving forward to your life plan dream when you feel as if you are wavering, drifting, or going off track.

Stephen Curry is generally regarded as the greatest shooter in the history of the National Basketball Association and is credited with revolutionizing the game by demonstrating that developing proficiency in the three-point shot and building a team's offense around it could translate into championship basketball. He proved that a game that had previously been dominated by physically imposing players with incredible athletic ability could be transformed into a game where an average-size player with good athletic ability but incredible ball-handling skills and otherworldly shooting ability could be the best player. Curry has led the league in scoring twice, is a four-time NBA champion, an NBA Finals MVP, and a two-time NBA regular season MVP. He is the only player in NBA history to win the MVP award on a unanimous vote. Curry did not become the NBA's greatest shooter by luck; he worked and worked and worked at it and then worked some more. He has taken tens of thousands of practice shots over the course of his time following his plan to pursue his dream of being the best shooter ever. However, even if you love basketball and your dream is to be the best player, there are times when you need something extra to help keep you going with a repetitive training activity of shooting a basketball over and over.

Curry uses a form of gamification to provide the additional extrinsic motivation he needs to stay passionately on track and laser focused. According to Andrew Lynch from Fox Sports in his article "This Is the Ridiculous Shooting Drill Steph Curry Uses to Crush the NBA," Curry sometimes uses a game called Beat the Ogre to challenge himself to stay sharp and overcome boredom.[3] When you are the best shooter of all time,

---

[3] Andrew Lynch, "This Is the Ridiculous Shooting Drill Steph Curry Uses to Crush the NBA," Fox Sports, March 14, 2016, www.foxsports.com/stories/nba/this-is-the-ridiculous-shooting-drill-steph-curry-uses-to-crush-the-nba.

normal drills can get old fast. In fact, Curry is known to have made seventy-seven straight three-point shots and ninety-four out of one hundred in a traditional practice shooting drill. Most of the people who were there would not have believed it if they didn't see it firsthand. When you have built such a high-proficiency skill over time, you need something a little extra to keep you interested at times.

According to Lynch's article, the rules of Beat the Ogre dictate that Curry shoots a series of NBA three-point shots while he is on the move, not a stationary set shot like traditional shooting practice drills. This is a game that Curry is playing against himself, and the objective is to score twenty-one points. The scoring rules of the game are that every three-pointer made is worth only one point and that every miss counts for negative four points. Thus, one miss wipes out four makes in the blink of an eye. Just to put this in perspective, if he misses his first three in a game of Beat the Ogre, he'll have to make thirty-three three-pointers in a row to win, and if he misses one, that results in four more in a row he has to make. Even with just one miss, he'll need to make twenty-five of twenty-six shots, or 96 percent, to win.

This is a great example of leveraging gamification to add additional fuel, motivation, and energy when needed to keep the activate perpetual cycle moving to continually grind to make your life plan a reality. Strategic time management provides the time allocation, planning, and discipline to support the laser focus model by actively managing time as a finite resource that again coupled with the internal strength developed in the A-attitudes of leadership capabilities should keep the cycle perpetually moving forward toward your life plan goals regardless of disruptions. But as mentioned before, there are times when you will need a turbocharge or jolt of electricity to overcome obstacles, monotony, and internal lethargy, and the gamification process provides an approach to accomplish this.

Key Steps of the Gamification Process

1. Begin by referring to your desired destiny life plan to remind yourself what inspired you to start this journey and what you are striving and sacrificing for.
2. Then refer to your personal laser focus model and your supplementary strategic time management model.
3. Allocate personal treats or rewards by score and time frame in both the laser focus model and the strategic time management model scorecards.
4. Leverage these extrinsic rewards as a complement to your intrinsic inspiration to stay on track, achieve your life plan dream, and control your destiny. Be authentic and hold yourself accountable to earn the rewards.

The bottom line is that the gamification process establishes formalized supplements to your intrinsic motivation by leveraging self-competition and extrinsic rewards to continually fuel the activate perpetual cycle. The extrinsic motivation may be in the form of physical rewards, or, as in the case of Steph Curry, it could be in the form of self-actualization. The form isn't what's important; instead, it's whether you see or feel it as something that gives you renewed energy and inspiration to relentlessly pursue your life plan's desired destiny.

ACTIVATION DRIVES TRANSFORMATION

Typically, great activation follows strong inspiration and engagement with a clear plan that lights the way, but there are times when activation is so powerful in and of itself that it becomes the fuel for an astonishing transformation. A good example is when I led my international operations team to undertake a massive performance improvement challenge in a large US multinational company several years ago. As in my other past roles, my priority was to get to know the organization by visiting all of our international sites to understand the businesses, technologies, and systems but more importantly to meet the people and experience the cultures. This would enable me to make connections and build relationships while also assessing our strengths, opportunities, and challenges.

After completing the visits, it became apparent that our international sites were far behind our domestic sites in overall performance as well as in safety, capability development, and standard processes. They also lacked inspiration, engagement, and a unified vision and seemed disconnected from the company. Finally, it appeared that they did not see themselves as valued members of the team. We needed a strategy that would not only dramatically improve performance but also inspiration, engagement, process standardization, and leadership capability development.

I introduced the concept of leveraging the iLEAD change model to drive our transformation. I met with local leaders and explained how I believed we could transform our sites to be world class and detailed how we would implement the iLEAD change model in the first half of the year to accelerate our progress. Our leaders were inspired and committed and were all in to lead by example, which was critical for an efficient rollout. The next step was to train them on the iLEAD change process so that they could activate the plan themselves at their respective sites. However, after the first training meeting, it became very clear that due to several factors like language challenges and lack of leadership experience and on-site role models, the local leaders did not know what the key aspects of the iLEAD change model actually looked like—namely, inspiration, light, and engagement—and thus could not lead by example. Even when they understood the translation, activating was not something they could envision, much less do or coach, because the concepts were not familiar to what they had experienced.

At this point I realized what I had to do, which was to personally coach our local leaders at every international site by modeling the iLEAD change process in person. This was a daunting commitment, because it meant I had to cover more than ten thousand team members in forty total sites across fifteen countries, speaking at least ten different languages in six months. This may not seem that difficult on the surface, but when you consider that I needed a minimum of two days at each site to train the leaders and model for them on the production shop floor, another two to four days to account for international travel, and another one to five days of intra-country travel because many of our sites were located in rural geographies, the complexity and time required quickly adds up. I committed to go to every site but asked six of my team members if they would be willing to divide the sites among themselves so that at least two of them would be with me at every visit to ensure that we had enough coaches to model and train everyone effectively and efficiently without overwhelming my team. They all were inspired and engaged by the vision and agreed.

Based on our initial plan, we would have to travel almost 170 of the 182 total days available, or about 90 percent of the next six months. This was clearly not practical, but we still were determined to find a way to make it happen and to inspire a positive cultural improvement. We needed to quickly improve safety for our people and performance for the company, but we also wanted everyone at our international locations to know that they mattered and were an important part of our team and organization, regardless of their location. We wanted everyone to feel that they were engaged in our transformation to world class and inspired by our commitment, passion, and sacrifice of being truly accessible and showing authentic adoration to them. We wanted to make a difference, so we decided to move forward anyway.

The only way we were going to able to pull off this logistical miracle was to stringently leverage the activate perpetual cycle. We started with laser focus by developing an overall plan, strategy, and timeline. We mapped out the travel to ensure that we could get to all forty sites in the time allotted in a way that would allow us to still be fresh and inspirational at every location but also preserve some semblance of work-life balance. Additionally, I reset our team's objectives and priorities for the next six months to be fully focused on this rollout plan.

We then developed a strategy to deal with the ten different languages, which included translating the training content to each one and hosting pre-visit virtual meetings to walk through the material and answer questions. For non-English locations, we doubled the virtual meeting time to allow for all content to be presented in their home language and assigned bilingual translators to facilitate content discussion and understanding as well as the translation of questions and answers. We also strategically divided the site leadership teams into three training groups for the on-site modeling visits and assigned each of us to lead a group based on our language proficiency and familiarity with the location.

Regarding strategic time management, we developed very detailed travel itineraries that encompassed all aspects of our visits down to the minute. To meet with and train people across forty sites in six months, we had to limit our stay at each location to fewer than two days and fully optimize that time. We did this by pre-aligning with the sites on the agenda and logistics as well as planning for rigorous schedule management during the visit using SMS text, WhatsApp, and WeChat for real-time communication and alerts. Most importantly, we aligned with the sites that we would cover all three shifts by coming in at 5:00 a.m. and staying through to 6:00 p.m. This would allow us to cover in one thirteen-hour day what would normally take two eight-hour days and be accessible to all three shifts for one-to-one sessions, small group and town hall meetings, and other informal connections, magnifying our opportunity to inspire and engage by a factor of three.

We wholeheartedly leveraged gamification to provide us with some extra motivation to stay focused and on schedule. We would engage the local teams to select the most authentic and culturally enriching restaurants for dinner each night, thus providing more opportunities to build deep relationships. We always requested the restaurants to be as culturally authentic as possible, which honored and surprised them because other corporate executives always preferred cuisines closer to their own. If we did not accomplish our objectives or dramatically went over schedule, we would lose this reward and not go. We never missed because of objectives, but we did go over schedule on a few occasions due to spending additional time with the people in the facilities; in some of our locations, that meant the equivalent of a convenience store dinner or possibly none at all. Not quite a reward, but these were conscious decisions to double down on accessibility and adoration where and when we felt it was necessary.

We also leveraged gamification when weekend stays were required, which was quite often. Similarly, we would engage the local team to suggest the most culturally impactful places for us to visit, sites to see, and things to do, but we would go only if we met our objectives for the week. Some were famous bucket list attractions like the Great Wall of China and the Eiffel Tower while others, unknown to most foreigners, provided genuinely unique experiences that were culturally priceless. Many times local team members would volunteer to accompany us, partly to build deeper relationships but also because they were proud to share their culture with us when most other executives never even asked and certainly wouldn't sacrifice their weekends for it.

This was still a monumental undertaking, but by leveraging the activate perpetual cycle, we were able to do it, giving us the opportunity to demonstrate to our international teams how much they mattered to us. We were able to get our travel down to 70 percent, which was still very high but tolerable for my team, since they were able to share the load. For me, I felt as the leader that it was critical to be present and to personally coach at each location. During that six-month period, I missed celebrating my wife's, son's, youngest daughter's, and my birthday; Mother's Day and Father's Day; Easter; Memorial Day; the Fourth of July; and fifteen weekends with my family. But the sacrifice was worth it. We were determined to make a difference, and a dramatic difference we made.

This work made a difference in inspiration, engagement, and commitment that drove an incredible culture and performance transformation much faster than even I anticipated. Almost immediately, our teams' engagement scores significantly increased to the highest in the entire company regardless of function, geography, and designation of headquarters versus field. But the transformation didn't stop there, as the sites continued to improve their activation of the iLEAD change model, and we saw dramatic improvements in safety and performance as well. The sites generated an 80 percent reduction in injuries, going from the highest to the lowest in the company, while also generating a 50 percent increase in manufacturing productivity and almost $100 million in incremental savings. Our teams were inspired by our vision and sacrifice to make it happen, engaged by our genuine interest and valuing of them and their cultures, and touched by our on-site coaching investment in their development, but it was the sacrifice of our activation that truly demonstrated our care, making the difference and fueling this astonishing transformation.

SUMMARY: iLEAD CHANGE *ACTIVATE*

Activate, as part of the iLEAD change model, is defined as the process of developing and activating, or bringing to life, the detailed plan to achieve your vision and goals to control your destiny. Even if your life plan is authentic and assured and includes a thorough, detailed plan, it will not achieve what you want if you don't hold yourself accountable to activate it.

Activate is about planning to win by not failing to plan or, said another way, developing the strategies that will earn success and clearly identifying, sequencing, and delivering the milestones to achieve your goals. As LeBron James said, "Nothing is given. Everything is earned." And iLEAD change *activate* is about earning the success you envision for yourself. The activate perpetual cycle is designed to help you earn that success by providing a structured approach to delivering your life plan milestones on an ongoing basis without interruption in a continuous and ordered cycle. It is comprised of the laser focus model that provides the process rigor and routine, the strategic time management model that provides the time allocation planning, and the gamification process that supplements intrinsic motivation by leveraging self-competition and extrinsic rewards.

CHAPTER 25

THE iLEAD CHANGE MODEL: DEVELOP

Develop, as part of the iLEAD change model, is defined as the process of growth through successive learning and the building of capability to continuously expand, differentiate, and evolve knowledge, perspective, and experience. Building continuous learning into your life plan is critically important. I call this having a Development Delta, or Dev-Delta, core mindset, which is about understanding that the more you know, the more you realize you don't know and about viewing all experiences, including failures, as positive learning opportunities to progressively transform. As stated in section 3, the Destiny Development Delta model is continuously evolving to keep you on track to achieve your long-term life goals. *Destiny* is the future state of your life and legacy that you are striving for, *development* is the never-ending learning and capability building we must have to grow and adapt, and *delta* represents our personal transformation and the ongoing dynamic changes that we face in our lives and in the world every day.

FIGURE 25.1: THE iLEAD CHANGE MODEL–DEVELOP

For the Destiny Development Delta model to optimally deliver, you must internalize a Dev-Delta core mindset in everything you do. This is imperative not only because it drives you to constantly learn and build your capability to control your destiny but also because it will build differential competitive advantage. If we were to consider the average amount of time that people typically spend on social media compared to the amount of time they dedicate to developing themselves by learning new skills, capabilities, and meaningful expertise, it would be clear that a Dev-Delta core mindset is not the norm or a priority for the majority of the population.

In fact, according to a recent study that appeared on BroadbandSearch.net, people spend on average 147 minutes each day on social media, which is almost two and a half hours per day. The article goes on to calculate that using the World Health Organization estimate of global life span to be seventy-three years, the average person will spend ten years or more of their lifetime on social media.[4] By contrast, according to the 2023 American Time Use Survey by the US Bureau of Labor Statistics, the average American spends about sixteen minutes per day reading for personal interest, or about a quarter of an hour.[5] Thus, the average American will spend fewer than six months of their lifetime reading for personal interest and development.

Consider the impact if a person reversed this dynamic and spent at least two and a half hours reading, learning, and developing themselves every day and only a quarter of an hour on social media. There is no question in my mind that ten years of incremental learning and self-development would be a significant competitive advantage for that person.

Certainly, two and a half hours per day developing oneself would be great, but some of the most successful people in the world have demonstrated that even if you dedicate fewer than half that time, it is still a tremendous competitive advantage that builds the Dev-Delta core mindset needed to achieve great things. According to the Entreprenuer.com article "The 5-Hour Rule Used by Bill Gates, Jack Ma and Elon Musk" by John Rampton, "The most successful people on the planet are also the people most likely to devote an hour a day to reading and learning."[6] Other very successful people who also heavily leverage reading and continuous learning include President Barack Obama, Mark Cuban, Oprah Winfrey, and Warren Buffett. According to Rampton, "The five-hour rule was coined by Michael Simmons, founder of Empact, who has written about it widely. The concept is wonderfully simple: No matter how busy successful people are, they always spend at least an hour a day—or five

---

4   Lyndon Seitz, "Average Daily Time Spent on Social Media (Latest 2024 Data)," Broadband-Search.net, April 18, 2024, www.broadbandsearch.net/blog/average-daily-time-on-social-media.

5   American Time Use Survey, "Average Hours Per Day Spent in Primary Activities for the Civilian Population, 2023 Quarterly and Annual Averages," US Bureau of Labor Statistics, last modified June 27, 2024, www.bls.gov/news.release/atus.t12.htm.

6   John Rampton, "The 5-Hour Rule Used by Bill Gates, Jack Ma and Elon Musk," Entrepreneur, November 4, 2019, www.entrepreneur.com/living/the-5-hour-rule-used-by-bill-gates-jack-ma-and-elon-musk/317602.

hours a workweek—learning or practicing. And they do this across their entire career."[7]

It should be clear by now that adopting the Dev-Delta core mindset is imperative to constantly learn and build your capability to strive for excellence and control your destiny. If you want to achieve the success you desire, you must continue to invest in yourself and put in the work. LeBron James put it this way: "Success isn't owned; it's leased. And the rent is due every day." If you want to be successful, pay your Development Delta rent every day.

Having a Dev-Delta core mindset will create a competitive advantage by continually building and upgrading your capability and capacity and be a key enabler of your life plan achievement. It's not how good you are but how good you want to be that matters. Pelé, arguably the greatest soccer player in history, summed it up well: "Success is no accident. It is hard work, perseverance, learning, studying, sacrifice and most of all, love of what you are doing or learning to do."

Over the next several pages, we'll provide general descriptions and presentations of the iLEAD change *develop* processes and models, integrated with personal stories to bring the Dev-Delta core mindset to life.

Personal Development Delta Plan Process

The personal Development Delta plan focuses on individual development of skills, capabilities, expertise, and experiences that must be gained to support milestone achievements and to progressively climb toward your desired destiny life plan. Best-selling author Malcolm Gladwell wrote *Outliers: The Story of Success* in 2008 and introduced the ten-thousand-hour rule, which basically stated that to develop a world-class skill or capability, it takes focused practice on that skill for ten thousand hours, or an average of twenty hours per week for ten years.[8] Whether this rule is 100 percent correct or not, it is difficult to argue that having a structured plan to improve and develop skills and

---

7 Rampton, "The 5-Hour Rule."
8 Malcolm Gladwell, *Outliers: The Story of Success* (New York: Little, Brown), 2008.

capabilities that are important enablers and milestones to achieve life goals and consistently activating that plan through practice and hard work will greatly enhance your chances for success. This is what the personal Development Delta plan is all about, providing a structured and strategic process aligned with your life plan to methodically and additively build and improve the skills and capabilities you need to make your destiny happen.

I talked about Steph Curry in the prior chapter in terms of how he leverages gamification to supplement his intrinsic motivation to continue to build his proficiency in shooting, even though he is already regarded as the greatest shooter in the history of the National Basketball Association. But how did he become the best shooter of all time? According to Scott Davis, in the *Business Insider* article "How Stephen Curry Became the Best Shooter the NBA Has Ever Seen," Curry benefited from the fact that his dad, Dell Curry, played in the NBA and was a great shooter.[9] Steph probably also benefited uniquely from nature in terms of shooting genes from his dad, from nurture by having a great shooter like his father teach him, and from being around basketball since he was born. It is important to note that he is not the only offspring of former NBA players who have had these nature and nurture advantages, but he is the only one to become the best shooter of all time. What did he do differently to develop himself into the very best? Davis provides the key points of Steph's differential development. I have listed them next, along with my commentary relating to the personal Development Delta plan.

- "He's hard-working and fiercely competitive."[10] He had the Dev-Delta core mindset of wanting to compete and be the best. Even though he is not the biggest, fastest, or strongest, he worked extremely hard on his shooting and was not afraid to miss, and he always played to win with a killer instinct on

---

9   Scott Davis, "How Stephen Curry Became the Best Shooter in the NBA," *Business Insider*, June 4, 2015, www.businessinsider.com/how-stephen-curry-became-best-shooter-in-the-nba-2015-6.
10   Davis, "How Stephen Curry Became the Best Shooter."

the court. Understanding that the path to learning and winning is being willing to fail is also key to the Dev-Delta core mindset.

- "He re-taught himself how to shoot in high school to adapt to bigger, better players."[11] His growth spurt came late, so in high school he had to adjust and compensate by changing aspects of his shooting technique that he had perfected over many years. This is very difficult physically and mentally, and many players have failed attempting to do this. As stated earlier, the world around you will change, so you must have the Dev-Delta core mindset of adaptability to keep your life plan dynamic and to quickly adjust to these changes.

- "He uses an insane 'flashing lights' test to work on his ball-handling while improving his reflexes and focus. He practices a combination of fundamentals and extremely detailed footwork that allows him to move, get into rhythm, and be ready to shoot easily and quickly."[12] Always finding more advanced training techniques to obtain a competitive advantage while continuing to challenge himself is a common trait that people striving to be the greatest have in common. This is another important aspect of the Dev-Delta core mindset, which is living by the fact that if you are not improving, you are declining. There is no maintaining.

- "Finally, Curry gets up plenty of shots."[13] There is no substitute for basic practice and repetition of the fundamentals that underpin your area of focus. Curry gets up hundreds of shots per day and thousands per year in practice. Fundamentals sometimes are the hardest to practice because it is easy for boredom and monotony to set in. This is why it is so important to ensure that you are truly authentic in selecting your desired destiny. Curry loves basketball, but even he has to find ways to stay interested

---

11 Davis, "How Stephen Curry Became the Best Shooter."
12 Davis, "How Stephen Curry Became the Best Shooter."
13 Davis, "How Stephen Curry Became the Best Shooter."

by using gamification in the form of drills like Beat the Ogre. The key to building the Dev-Delta core mindset and to activating it, like Steph Curry, is to ensure that you are authentically focused on a destiny you want and love so that you will want and love to put in the work.

Although Steph Curry did not employ the exact personal Development Delta plan presented here, this example illustrates the objective of what the process is designed to do, which is to methodically build the skills and capabilities needed to make your destiny happen. It focuses on your individual development, enabling you to differentiate yourself and create sustained competitive advantage. A recent survey indicated that only 54 percent of all working Americans and 61 percent of those under thirty think it will be essential to develop new skills throughout their working lives.[14] According to a report by McKinsey, up to 375 million workers worldwide will need to change roles or learn new skills by 2030.[15]

As mentioned earlier, the average American spends only about sixteen minutes per day on reading for personal interest. We can extrapolate this to mean that not much more time is spent than this on overall self-development focused on achieving long-term goals. Reading is only one aspect of self-development; others include learning a second or third language, practicing public speaking, improving writing, enhancing problem-solving and logic skills, and so on. I think it is safe to estimate that based on the sixteen minutes of reading per day estimate, most Americans likely spend fewer than thirty minutes per day in total on self-development as part of a structured plan with the strategic focus of establishing building blocks to achieve long-term life plan goals.

---

14 Pew Research Center, "The State of American Jobs," October 6, 2016, www.pewresearch.org/social-trends/2016/10/06/the-state-of-american-jobs.
15 Raphael Bick, Eric Hazan, Hamza Khan, Sebastien Lacroix, Hugo Sarrazin, and Tom Welchman, "The Future of Work: Reskilling and Remote Working to Recover in the 'Next Normal,'" McKinsey & Company, June 25, 2020, https://mck.co/3WUokqu.

This is unfortunate because having a structured process like the personal Development Delta plan, along with the discipline to activate, is one of the most surefire ways to differentiate yourself and achieve your goals, by putting in the work and grinding every day while others are prioritizing more unstructured or leisure activities. Like it or not, it's inevitable that you will face the duality of competing against yourself in terms of overcoming feelings of monotony, impatience, skepticism, and boredom and against others in terms of accomplishments, jobs, legacy, and the like as you strive to achieve your desired destiny. Having a structured personal Development Delta plan to go along with the Dev-Delta core mindset to activate it will give you a competitive advantage. Pelé said in relation to this, "I used to train very hard. When the other players went to the beach after training, I was there kicking the ball."

How do you feel about the amount of structured time and focus you are allocating to your own development?

The personal Development Delta plan process is the most important tool for iLEAD change *develop* because it is the overall process for strategically driving one's development. Figure 25.2 shows this process, followed by a description of each step and a few personal stories to bring it to life.

FIGURE 25.2: PERSONAL DEVELOPMENT DELTA PLAN PROCESS

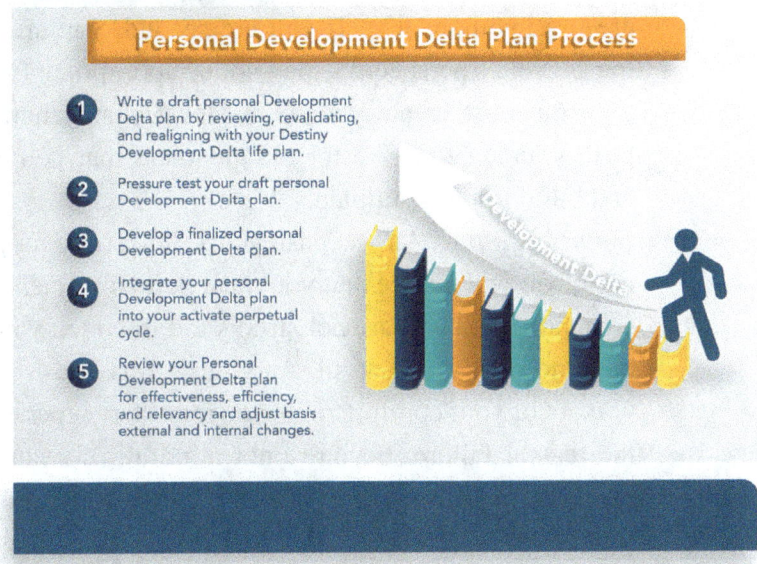

The Personal Development Delta Plan Process

1. *Write a draft personal Development Delta plan by reviewing, revalidating, and realigning with your life plan.* You must ensure that you are focusing on your authentic desired destiny that you want and love so that you will want and love to put in the work to continually develop yourself.
2. *Pressure test your draft personal Development Delta plan.* Assess whether each of the items on your draft list is a critical priority to achieving your life plan goals and gauge whether your development plan and proficiency targets are of adequate stretch and challenge. As part of the pressure test, it is critical to hold yourself accountable to address the following three key points:

- *Strive for greatness.* Remember that the Dev-Delta core mindset includes the idea that if you are not improving, you are declining. Pelé would push himself with a core value accountability characterized by this quote: "If you are first, you are first. If you are second, you are nothing."[43] Pelé's perspective may not be appropriate for you, but you must create your own Dev-Delta mentality to push yourself to strive for the greatness that you define and build it into your plan.
- *Embrace failure.* As you push yourself to strive for greatness, you will realize that you must build proficiencies in areas in which you are not strong and in which you may have no experience at all. As you do this and it moves you out of your comfort zone, you may start experiencing the fear of failure. If you're not mindful, this can paralyze you or cause you to hesitate, either consciously or subconsciously, to add stretch development to your plan. Being willing to fail is the fastest path to learning and winning, and this is critically important to a Dev-Delta core mindset. Two of the greatest athletes in the world know this well and profess to this core value. LeBron James's perspective on embracing failure is characterized in these two quotes: "You can't be afraid to fail. It's the only way you succeed" and "You have to be able to accept failure to get better." Serena Williams's perspective on losing is similarly characterized by this quote: "I don't like to lose—at anything . . . Yet I've grown most not from victories, but setbacks. If winning is God's reward, then losing is how he teaches us."[16] You must push yourself in building and activating your personal Development Delta plan while embracing the fact that you will make mistakes and experience setbacks but that

---

16 Fearless Motivation, "The Greatest Serena Williams Quotes."

they will be accelerating your learning. That which does not destroy you makes you stronger.
- *Cultivate feedback.* It's important to obtain external perspective on your strengths, opportunities, and weaknesses to build into or adjust your plan if needed. Cultivating feedback also underscores your commitment to the Dev-Delta core mindset by actively overcoming your fear and risk avoidance through demonstrating vulnerability and opening yourself to potential criticism, which is very difficult for most people to do and, if not overcome, hinders the capacity to learn. Many of the greatest among us, including the best athletes, artists, business leaders, and social entrepreneurs, have someone they trust, a personal coach, family member, colleague, or friend, who will tell them the truth about how they can get better.

3. *Develop a finalized personal Development Delta plan.* Refine your pressure-tested working list of key personal development objectives to a range of one to three for the near term and one to two each for medium and longer term. By following this process, you should have no more than seven development objectives in your plan, and this limited number should provide the capacity for you to fit into your activation plan. The near-term objectives are development items to complete within twelve months while the medium-term objectives should target one to three years and the longer-term greater than three years. This is important because there will be high-priority development objectives that will take multiple years to complete but that must be integrated into your activation plan to ensure that they stay on track. A perfect example is the pursuit of an advanced educational degree, which requires planning, work, and focus over several years and must be built into your plan.

4. *Integrate your personal Development Delta plan into your activate perpetual cycle.* This ensures that your personal

Development Delta objectives will have adequate focus and time allotment without sacrificing other parts of your overall life plan, including your personal well-being and holistic balance.

5. *Review your personal Development Delta plan for effectiveness, efficiency, and relevancy and adjust based on external and internal changes.* Formally review your plan and make appropriate adjustments quarterly, as well as informally daily and weekly, as part of the laser focus model because the speed of external change in the world today is lightning fast. Remember, the entire world changed in fewer than three months due to an unforeseen global pandemic. Continue to build your Dev-Delta core mindset to always be prepared to adjust and adapt to keep your life plan on track.

PERSONAL DEVELOPMENT DELTA PLAN PROCESS STORIES

Earning My MBA

In early 1994, I decided to pursue my Master of Business Administration just a few months after the birth of our second child. I had also just received a big promotion to lead at one of the largest food production operations in the world. Additionally, I was only two years removed from completing my Master of Science degree at Purdue University. On the surface, it may not have seemed to make sense to go back to graduate school with two small kids at home, a big new job, only two years in the workforce, and a graduate degree already to my credit. But earning an MBA was an important milestone in my personal Development Delta plan toward achieving my desired destiny.

As part of my life plan, I had a career goal to become a CEO or a C-suite executive at a Fortune 500 company. I knew that to achieve this goal, I would need accelerated business experience, acumen, and expertise. I also knew that although I was going to get significant leadership development in my new job as the leader of a large complex operation, I would not have significant exposure to the overall business model and corporate structure. My assumption was that I would probably be in this role for at least three years before moving to a corporate position, more than likely still in operations instead of marketing, finance, or other commercial parts of the business. From my perspective, accelerating my business education, acumen, and expertise by earning my MBA as soon as possible was a smart move.

But there were other factors to consider, the most important being my family. It was imperative to maintain our holistic balance and well-being. My wife and I had only been recently married, and we had a two-year-old and a baby at home. I asked her opinion on whether I should pursue my MBA now or wait. We discussed the pros and cons and decided together that if I was going to do it, this would be the best time, while the kids were small. We knew that it would be a huge commitment and sacrifice, but we were resolute that we could get through the next eighteen months together.

Next, I considered the appropriate choice of university. I received a lot of advice that I should be targeting the very best business schools. But based on my life plan and my intent to minimize any negative impact to my family, I questioned that. It would be great to attend a top ten business school, but was it worth it to quit my job, lose my income for two years, and uproot my family to do it? As I reassessed my life plan, I realized that the prestige of the university was not the most important factor because, among other reasons, I already had a master's degree from a prestigious school, I was a top-level performer at a Fortune 500 company, and I had proven that I was an inspirational leader. Additionally, I had the confidence that it would not be the name of the university on my MBA that would get me the top job or a C-suite executive position but my vision, leadership, and ability to inspire and engage. The MBA would simply be an accelerator to building my business expertise and credibility.

I then had to decide whether to go full time. I wanted to complete the MBA program as quickly as possible and minimize any negative impact to my young family, maintaining our holistic balance and personal well-being. Additionally, as I said, I wanted to continue working full time to take on the challenges of the new job and maintain my income to take care of my family. The question was: Could I find a program that was not only close to my home but also allowed me to both work and study full time? There was only one school at the time that met these qualifications. Nova Southeastern University offered a cluster-learning, eighteen-month, full-time MBA program, whereby they flew professors into a location every other weekend to teach a cluster or cohort of about twenty MBA students. Remember that this was before the internet, so there was no virtual option or Zoom classroom. This cluster-learning program was pretty revolutionary at the time to support people who wanted to pursue their MBA full time while maintaining full-time employment and not totally disrupting or uprooting families. Nova Southeastern University had a cluster that met twenty minutes from my house.

I knew that pursuing my MBA as a full-time student while working full time leading a large and complex operation was going to be extremely challenging and fraught with potential failure, but I embraced the risks and flipped the thought of failure to the reality of accelerated learning and personal growth. I registered for Nova Southeastern University's full-time program, and after completing eighteen of the hardest and most stressful but also most incredibly developmental months of growth in my life, I graduated in May 1996 and later accepted a big promotion with another company that accelerated my life plan forward.

It turned out to be a great decision for me, as the knowledge I gained from earning my MBA enhanced my business acumen, and the experience of studying for it while successfully leading a large complex operation reaffirmed my confidence that I could control my destiny if I continued to take on challenges, embrace the potential for failure, and build my Dev-Delta core mindset.

Learning Additional Languages

Another example from my personal Development Delta plan is my milestone commitment to learning additional languages. This was an important part of my life plan for several reasons, including pushing me out of my comfort zone and challenging me to continuously learn, opening more career opportunities, and enabling me to build a more expansive and diverse network.

Many people believe that learning a secondary language is not easy. For most of us, it does take a lot of work, diligence, and patience as well as the courage to practice it. To successfully pursue a language to the point of proficiency, you must have the authentic drive to hold yourself accountable to start learning and speaking it. Learning Spanish was in my life plan from the beginning, but it wasn't until I was forty-one years old and my responsibilities expanded to include a large team in Mexico that I decided to formally commit to integrate it into my activate perpetual cycle, learn it, and, more importantly, force myself to use it. I requested that my weekly performance review conference calls with the Mexico team and my bi-monthly site visits to Mexico be in Spanish. This included one-to-one meetings and small group presentations. I even delivered town hall keynote addresses, including question and answer sessions, in Spanish, as well as our socializing time at breakfast, lunch and dinner. It was very hard and humbling. I made lots of mistakes and would have massive headaches every night from translating in my head all day. But I was driven to overcome the struggles and the fear and ultimately became business fluent.

A few years later, I committed to learning Portuguese. Again, my accountabilities had expanded, this time to include a recently acquired Brazilian business with six thousand team members. Similar to my Spanish learning experience, I forced myself to use Portuguese at every virtual and in-person business meeting with the Brazilian team. However, unlike Mexico, where we had only one site, we had twenty sites in Brazil spread across the country. Many were located in rural areas that were difficult to access, and traveling to them meant lots of driving and stops at roadside convenience stores and local coffee shops and restaurants. Now I was forced to stretch well beyond even my uncomfortable zone, because I had to adapt, speak, and try to understand everyday street Portuguese.

The biggest obstacle in learning languages is overcoming the fear of failure—making mistakes, sounding unprofessional, speaking in broken tongue, and feeling silly or stupid. This is why children can learn languages so much faster than adults, because the reward of making new friends and being included in play outweighs their fears. I embraced my discomfort and overcame my fear because I authentically wanted to speak the language, and I was self-assured that the best way to learn was to embrace my Dev-Delta core mindset and just do it. I spoke as much as I could with as many people as I could, and I made many mistakes and cultivated lots of feedback to accelerate my learning. It was interesting that people actually appreciated that I, as a leader and corporate executive, was willing to spend so much time to learn their language, making mistakes in front of them and being vulnerable.

There is no question that my commitment to learning languages has been key in enabling my life plan. It reinforced my A-attitudes of leadership development and accelerated my ability to build a global network of strong relationships and passionate supporters, dramatically expanding my leadership influence. It also strengthened my Dev-Delta core mindset by reinforcing that the rewards of continuous learning and adaptability are best enabled by embracing the fear of embarrassment, mistakes, and failure.

The Multilevel Mentor Model

The personal Development Delta plan is the most important enabler for iLEAD change *develop* because it represents the holistic process for aligning your overall continuous learning strategy with your life plan milestones. However, there are additional *develop* models and processes that provide more targeted support and development to complement your life plan. The multilevel mentor model is one of these. We use the term *multilevel mentor* to refer to a group of people representing truly diverse and disparate demographics that can provide differential knowledge, insight, perspective, and counsel that you might not otherwise attain to accelerate your Dev-Delta core mindset and the successful activation of your life plan.

There are multiple objectives in the multilevel mentor model. The first is to gain a more complete picture of how you are perceived across different groups. The second is acquiring targeted mentoring in specific areas to obtain unique expertise. The third is to actively stretch your thought process both horizontally, with far-reaching peer mentors, and vertically, with bidirectional mentors who may be perceived to be above or below you in age, experience, or some arbitrary societal hierarchy, to expose you to points of view, trends, and possibilities that would be practically invisible or unknown to you.

It is a big mistake to think that a mentor must be older or more successful than you. You should always be looking to recruit diverse people to add to your network of mentors and mentees. Anyone can be a mentor if they bring unique perspective, learnings, expertise, and points of view that either you don't have to their level or at all. Multilevel mentors who span your network horizontally and vertically accomplish all of that and will accelerate your learning capacity and Dev-Delta core mindset. Figure 25.3 presents the multilevel mentor model followed by a personal story to help bring it to life.

FIGURE 25.3: THE MULTILEVEL MENTOR MODEL

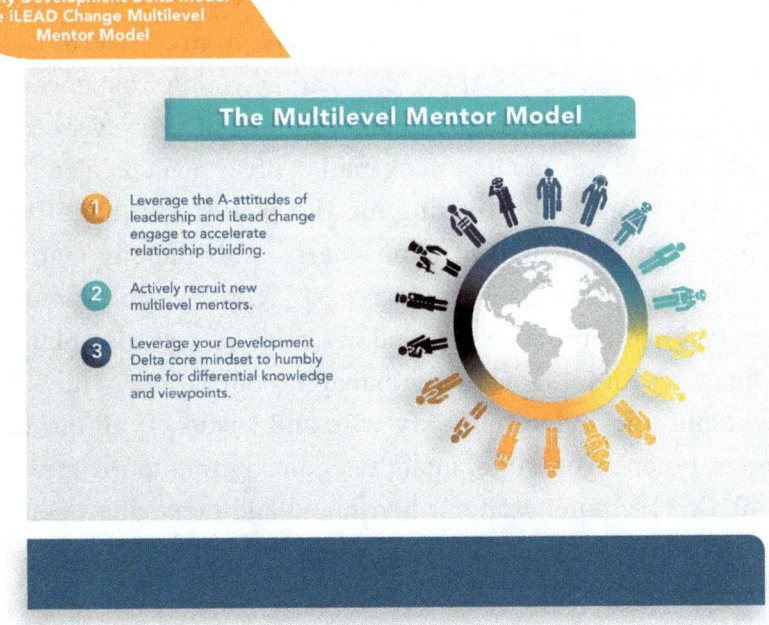

To assess how well you are leveraging multilevel mentors, evaluate the balance of your mentor network.

Think about all the key mentors in your life and list their names. Then think about the multilevel mentor model and draw a circle. For every mentor on your list, draw a stick figure to represent them in the top part of the circle if they would be considered senior or more advanced in their career or life than you (your parents, boss, religious leader, current or retired executive, etc.), in the middle part of the circle if they would be considered peers (your partner, colleague, classmate, etc.), and at the bottom part of the circle if they would be considered junior or less advanced in their career or life than you (your kids, employees, people in lower-level jobs or careers, etc.). A balanced network should have mentor figures evenly distributed around the circle. If your mentor network is not balanced, what actions will you take to remedy this?

THE MULTILEVEL MENTOR MODEL PERSONAL STORY

The Millionaire Janitor

Here is a personal story and example of the Destiny Development Delta multilevel mentor model. Mentors can come from anywhere in society. The key is to remember that you can learn anything from anyone if you integrate your Dev-Delta core mindset as part of your everyday life. A perfect example was my first stock market investment mentor.

A few years into activating my life plan, I felt that things were going really well. After only four years, I was happily married with three beautiful kids, had earned my MBA, had been promoted four times, and had more than doubled my salary. I was also planning for our financial future by actively managing our money with a detailed budget and tracking system. My wife and I paid off all our debt and saved as much as possible, including contributing to the max limit of my 401(k). We purchased our first home and then subsequently used that equity to trade up to a larger home. I thought we were covering all the bases.

At this time, I was managing a large technical operation of about four hundred highly skilled and well-compensated people. However, like most operations, there sometimes was a need for work that is still important but less technical, requires less skill, and is not as highly compensated. A good example of this is janitorial services, and one of the janitors in our operation was an older gentleman named LeRoy. He was probably in his mid-sixties at the time, and although he had been presented with many opportunities to be promoted to higher-skilled work in which he would earn more money, he remained a janitor.

I talked to LeRoy every day during my walks around the facility to assess the status of the operation and connect with the team members. LeRoy was a fairly quiet guy but always had a smile on his face and something to say about Michael Jordan and the Chicago Bulls (this was 1996, the heyday of the Bulls dynasty). I noticed that LeRoy always had a *Fortune* magazine in his back pocket. One day I asked him about it. He said, "Ah, you don't want to talk to me about this stuff. I'm just an old janitor. What do I know?" I told him I was genuinely interested. He then asked me if I had a few minutes to talk so that he could explain it in some detail.

We went into the break room, and he asked me, "Are you in the market? Do you own stocks?" I told him I had company stock and mutual funds in my 401(k). He laughed and then gave me a detailed lesson on investing in the stock market that would have put many financial advisers to shame. He explained to me who Warren Buffett was, whom at that time I had not heard of. He detailed the power of compound interest and the invest and hold strategy over time based on the long-term consistent growth of the stock market. He told me about his portfolio, which was worth over a million dollars, and his focus on only blue-chip stocks with strong balance sheets. He asked me to research his list of must-own stocks and think about how I would build my own portfolio, which we would discuss later that week.

That night I went home and did my research. I was blown away by the extent and quality of his investment strategy knowledge and recommendations. The next day when I saw LeRoy, I told him I checked out everything he said and that he was right on point. I liked his stock recommendations and added a few of my own and then asked if he had any additional advice to get me started. He said, "You know, you shocked me yesterday. I've carried that magazine in my back pocket for years, and nobody ever asked me anything about it. They probably thought I used it for a dustpan or something. But you asked and then you actually listened to me." He then told me that he was very happy and proud that I researched and liked his recommendations, but he counseled me to get a really good financial planner to set up my accounts the right way, especially considering my young family.

Over the next week, I hired a financial planner from a reputable firm, implemented many of LeRoy's recommendations, opened what at the time were called education IRAs (now 529 plans) for my kids' futures, and established an ongoing investment strategy with target goals and direct deposit funding. From that point forward, I dedicated at least two hours every Saturday to reviewing my portfolio, modeling future growth, reading about new stock ideas, and reviewing market strategies. Additionally, I would always allocate ten minutes or so a few days a week to have an extended conversation with LeRoy about the market, investments, and retirement planning and to get his advice and feedback on my progress.

I was the twenty-seven-year-old senior manager with two master's degrees while LeRoy was a janitor who had never even graduated from high school. But he had become my mentor when it came to investment knowledge and wealth-building strategies, not only because he was a smart and patient investor but also because I was open to learn from him regardless of his job, hierarchy in our operation, or other people's perception of him. I followed the multilevel mentor model by recognizing LeRoy as an equal and treating him with the value and respect he deserved. I actively opened the door to recruit LeRoy as a mentor by first noticing and asking about the *Fortune* magazine and then, more importantly, by being open to listen to him. Finally, I leveraged my Dev-Delta core mindset to check my ego and be humble enough to learn financial strategy from a janitor by recognizing and purposefully mining LeRoy's differential knowledge in investing and money management and establishing an open and trusting mentor relationship for cultivating feedback and advice.

SUMMARY: iLEAD CHANGE *DEVELOP*

Develop, as part of the iLEAD change model, is defined as the process of growth through successive learning and capability building to continuously expand, differentiate, and evolve knowledge, perspective, and experience. Having a Dev-Delta core mindset is about understanding that the more we know, the more we realize how much we don't know. It's viewing all experiences, including failures, as positive learning opportunities to progressively transform. *Develop* helps you to strive for excellence, creating differential competitive advantage.

We introduced two of the *develop* processes and models. The first is the personal Development Delta plan process, which is focused on individual skills, capabilities, and experiences that must be gained to support milestone achievement for your life plan. It's the most important tool for iLEAD change *develop* because it is the overall process for strategically driving your development. The second is the multilevel mentor model, which encompasses recruiting truly diverse mentors who provide insight, knowledge, or perspective that you might not otherwise attain to accelerate your Dev-Delta core mindset and the successful activation of your life plan.

SECTION 6

MILESTONE 3: THE FORMULA FOR SUCCESS

**Destiny Development Delta Model
The Three Major Milestones
of the Deployment Model
and Key Deliverables**

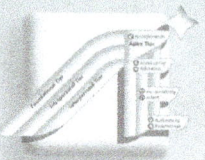

ATTITUDES
OF LEADERSHIP

The A-Attitudes of
Leadership Personal
Transformation Model

Holistic Balance and
Personal Well-being

The A-Attitudes of
Leadership Capability,
Development to Support
Your Transformation

iLEAD
CHANGE

Destiny Development
Delta Life Plan

iLEAD Change
Capability, Processes,
and Models to Activate
Your Life Plan

FORMULA
FOR SUCCESS

The Comprehensive
Destiny Development
Delta Model
Deployment Process

Progress Tracking
and Measurement
Assessment

Dedicated Coaching,
Mentoring, and Support

CHAPTER 26

MAIN MESSAGES OF SECTION 6

In this section, I will cover the following key summary points:

- The formula for success is the proprietary process to ensure that your adoption of the Destiny Development Delta model results in successful personal transformation and in the development and activation of your life plan. It is comprised of three principal aspects:

    1. The comprehensive Destiny Development Delta model deployment process
    2. Progress tracking and measurement assessment
    3. Dedicated coaching, mentoring, and support

- The comprehensive Destiny Development Delta model deployment process is the structured and systematic approach for deployment of the model.
- Progress tracking and measurement assessment are the proprietary assessment processes to gauge progress and identify gaps and areas of opportunity to fortify learning and ensure readiness to progress through the model deployment milestones.
- Dedicated coaching, mentoring, and support facilitates the personal transformation and construction of the life plan and translates the progress tracking into learning and capability adjustments as needed. It is the most critical aspect of the formula for success, as it guides the crucial year-one launch and activation of the life plan.

CHAPTER 27

THE FORMULA FOR SUCCESS

The objective of this section is to explain milestone 3 of the deployment process, which introduces the Destiny Development Delta formula for success.

The formula for success is the proprietary process to ensure that your adoption of the Destiny Development Delta model results in successful personal transformation and development and activation of your life plan. It is comprised of three principal aspects as illustrated in figure 27.1.

FIGURE 27.1: THE FORMULA FOR SUCCESS

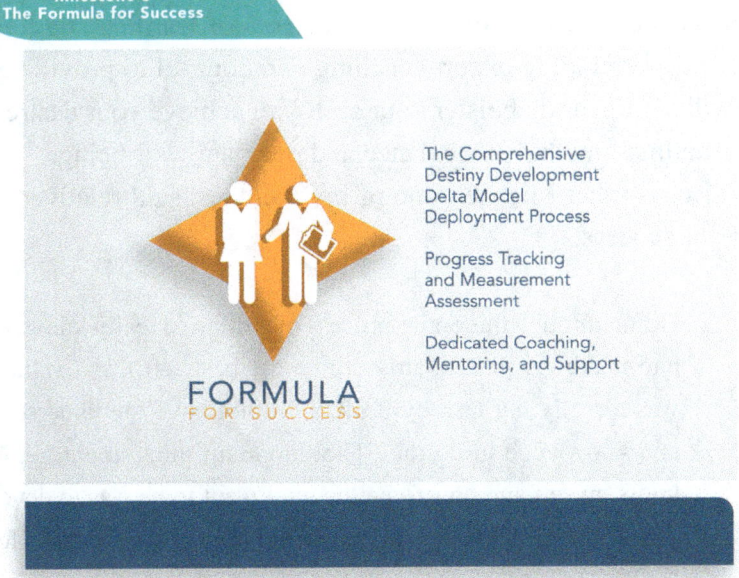

1. *The comprehensive Destiny Development Delta model deployment process* is the first aspect of the formula for success and is the structured and systematic approach for deployment of the model.
2. *Progress tracking and measurement assessment* are the proprietary assessment processes to gauge progress and identify gaps and areas of opportunity to fortify learning and ensure readiness to progress through the model deployment milestones.
3. *Dedicated coaching, mentoring, and support* facilitates the personal transformation and construction of the life plan and translates the progress tracking into learning and capability adjustments as needed. It is the most critical aspect of the formula for success, as it guides the crucially important year-one launch and activation of the life plan.

The intent of the formula for success is to gauge your deployment progress and identify gaps to inform the development of remediation plans to keep you on track. The three aspects work together to provide a thorough support approach. By completing the detailed Destiny Development Delta deployment process, including formally assessing progress at each checkpoint to ensure depth of learning and transformation while leveraging expert coaching and counsel to provide guidance, you will significantly bolster your ability to achieve your desired destiny while maintaining holistic balance and personal well-being.

Here is what Michael, one of my mentees, said relative to the formula for success:

> Going through this entire process of getting to really know myself and making a plan to strive to be the best self that I want to be was a really big task by itself. I did not have the understanding and knowledge to do this. The important thing about getting to know myself and how to be the me I want to be was to develop a plan to do this in a way that allowed me to grow, set goals for my

life, and be balanced. Following the Destiny Development Delta deployment model with the structured processes and the models and tools really was good, but the checkpoints for progress and the development contracts brought out my accountability to the process. But above all it is the personal coaching and investment in myself that is making the difference.

THE FORMULA FOR SUCCESS ASPECT 1:
THE COMPREHENSIVE DESTINY DEVELOPMENT DELTA MODEL DEPLOYMENT PROCESS

The first aspect of the formula for success is completing the comprehensive Destiny Development Delta model deployment process, which is the structured and systematic approach for deploying the Destiny Development Delta model.

FIGURE 27.2: THE FORMULA FOR SUCCESS ASPECT 1: THE COMPREHENSIVE DESTINY DEVELOPMENT DELTA MODEL DEPLOYMENT PROCESS

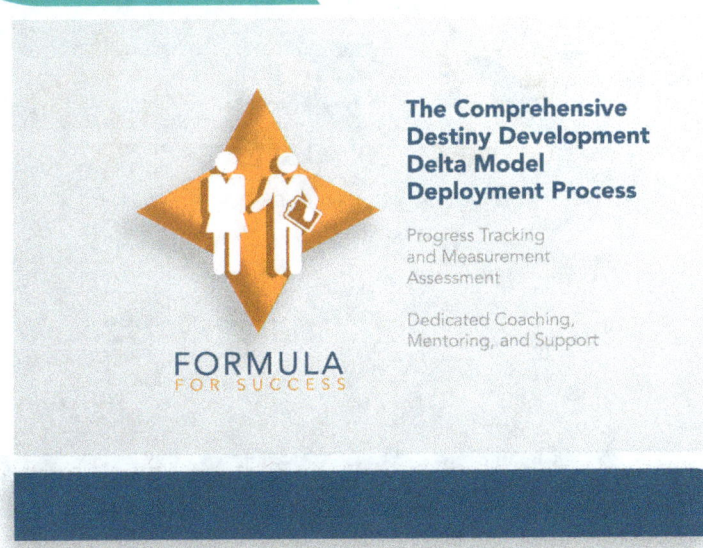

The Destiny Development Delta model drives a holistic personal transformation by integrating the A-attitudes of leadership and the iLEAD change capabilities into a truly holistic model that, when deployed to leverage our process, will guarantee your success. As explained in section 4, the deployment process for the integrated Destiny Development Delta model is comprised of the following three major milestones:

1. Milestone 1: Build A-attitudes of leadership capability to develop the holistic balance and personal well-being required to initiate and sustain your transformation.
2. Milestone 2: Build iLEAD change capability to create and activate your life plan.
3. Milestone 3: Leverage the formula for success to successfully launch the journey to take control of your destiny.

FIGURE 27.3: THE THREE MAJOR MILESTONES OF THE DESTINY DEVELOPMENT DELTA MODEL

The focus of these milestones is to provide a structured and systematic approach to ensure the most optimum integration of the A-attitudes of leadership with iLEAD change. The remainder of this chapter is dedicated to providing an overview of the contents and deliverables in each of the three major milestones for the deployment process.

Milestone 1
Milestone 1 is to build A-attitudes of leadership capability to develop the holistic balance and personal well-being required to initiate and sustain your transformation. This is achieved through development first in the foundational tier of authenticity and assuredness, second in the intrapersonal tier of action and accountability, third in the interpersonal tier of accessibility and adoration, and fourth in the apex tier of amalgamation, to converge with the iLEAD change model.

Milestone 2
Milestone 2 is to build iLEAD change capability to create and activate your life plan. The focus will be on establishing your desired destiny, building your life plan, and reliably activating it over time. This begins with *inspire*, which is focused on leveraging the deep self-awareness and development in the A-attitudes of leadership model in milestone 1 to identify your desired destiny and life plan that is true to yourself. The next section, *light*, is focused on creating the clarity of communication of your life plan so that you are successfully inspired to believe in your vision. *Engage* is the next section, which improves your capability to build networks and relationships and to leverage your clarity of communications to recruit passionate supporters. The penultimate section is *activate*, which is all about bringing your plan to life and making it happen over time to achieve your life plan goals. The final section is *develop*, which introduces the concept of the Development Delta core mindset of continuous learning to enable you to quickly adjust and adapt to stay on track as both planned and unplanned life, environmental, and social changes inevitably come your way.

Milestone 3

Milestone 3 is to leverage the formula for success to effectively launch the journey to take control of your destiny. This is the proprietary process to ensure that your adoption of the Destiny Development Delta model results in successful personal transformation and the development and activation of your life plan and sets you firmly on track to take control of your destiny.

These three milestones provide the systematic and structured approach for deploying the Destiny Development Delta model, differentiating it from all other models by guaranteeing your successful personal transformation as well as the construction and activation of your desired destiny life plan.

THE FORMULA FOR SUCCESS ASPECT 2: PROGRESS TRACKING AND MEASUREMENT ASSESSMENT

The second aspect of the Destiny Development Delta formula for success is progress tracking and measurement assessment, which is a proprietary process designed to gauge the level of personal transformation and capability development adequacy to take and sustain control of your destiny. It is about assessing the depth of the capability and confidence you are building to persevere and succeed over the long journey of the life plan.

FIGURE 27.4: THE FORMULA FOR SUCCESS ASPECT 2: PROGRESS TRACKING AND MEASUREMENT ASSESSMENT

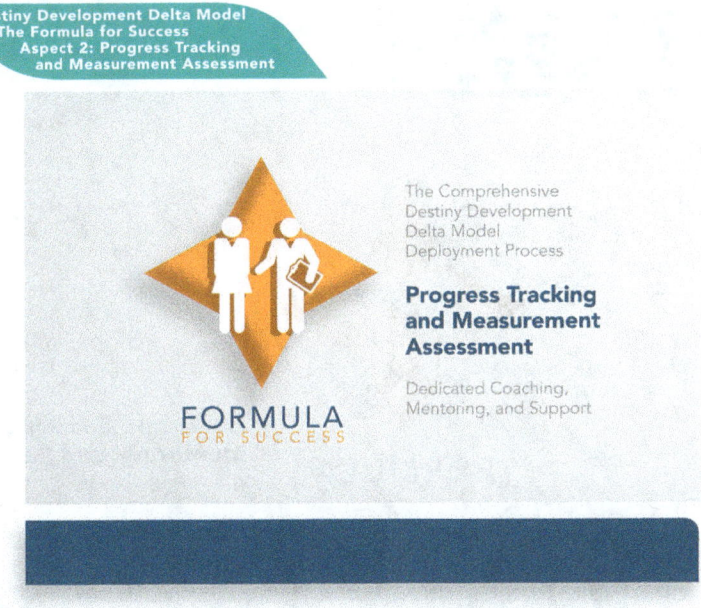

Progress tracking and measurement assessment has three checkpoints aligned with the first two deployment milestones, the A-attitudes of leadership and the iLEAD change models. Again, the intent is to ensure depth of transformation, learning, and understanding and to identify development opportunities.

THE FORMULA FOR SUCCESS ASPECT 3: DEDICATED COACHING, MENTORING, AND SUPPORT

The third aspect of the formula for success is dedicated coaching, mentoring, and support, which facilitates the personal transformation and construction of the life plan, translates the progress tracking into learning and capability adjustments as needed, and guides and coaches the critically important year-one launch and activation.

FIGURE 27.5: THE FORMULA FOR SUCCESS ASPECT 3: DEDICATED COACHING, MENTORING, AND SUPPORT

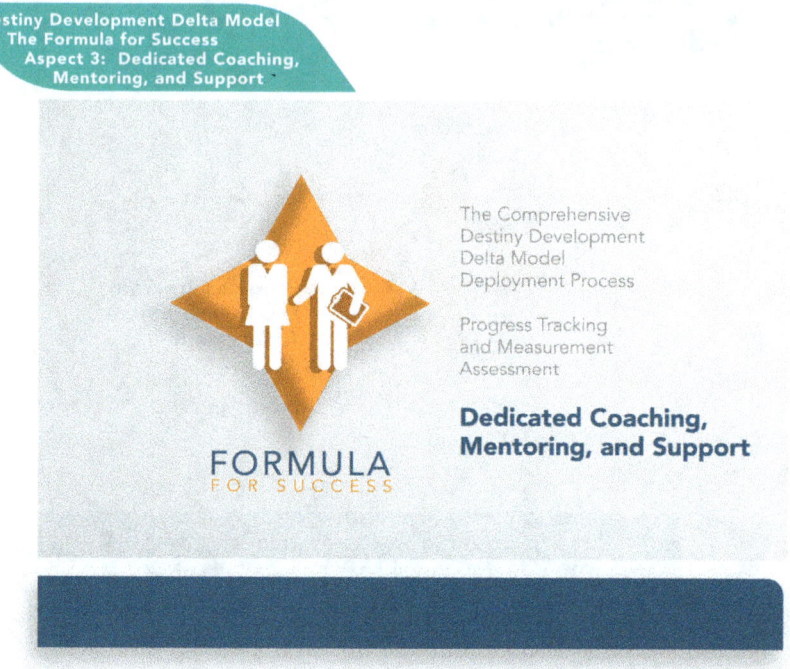

Dedicated coaching, mentoring, and support is the most critical aspect of the formula for success, especially in the first year of deploying the Destiny Development Delta model. Here is what one of my mentees, Li Na, said about this:

> Even for the most driven and confident of us, dedicated coaching can make a big difference. Actually, it can make the biggest difference if you have the right coach. Sometimes you can be comfortable in a certain area or aspect of your life or focused on only one path, and this can cause you to not be able to see the bigger or broader picture. For me, this is really important. There are certain things that I like to do, and I can get comfortable with

these things, but I also want to achieve my full potential as a professional and as a person. Donzel has and continues to coach me to see this bigger picture and proactively understand the trade-offs for getting outside my comfort zone to challenge myself to achieve my full potential, whether it is pushing me to think long term about where I want myself and my family to be or expanding my thought process to career opportunities that I normally would not consider or continually building my network of stakeholders and supporters. This is all critical, and having a coach who will tell me what I need to hear rather than what I might want to hear is most important.

Development in the A-attitudes of learning foundational tier of authenticity and assuredness to build your self-awareness, holistic balance, and personal well-being is critical to initiating your transformation journey. Attempting this heavy lifting on your own is extremely difficult and will more than likely be frustrating as well. Leveraging an expert coach to facilitate and guide you through the process will help you identify strengths, gaps, and areas where growth is needed. Accurately assessing yourself is hard because we tend to have built-in blinders to our gaps and sometimes to our strengths and weaknesses too. We also can at times fall victim to looking at ourselves through a distorted lens that artificially magnifies or minimizes strengths and weaknesses, thus giving us a false view.

The bottom line is that we are not the most reliable assessors and developers of ourselves. This is why some of the greatest athletes in the world have personal coaches, because they know that they must have a complete and 100 percent unbiased assessment of themselves in conjunction with strong and relentless push and targeted skill development in their areas of weaknesses and strengths to grow and achieve their full potential. Whether it's NBA players or UEFA Champions League footballers, they are all leveraging personal trainers and coaches to help attain their goals. According to the March 30, 2020, article "From Cristiano Ronaldo to Odion Ighalo—Footballers Depend on Personal Trainers to Be Their Best" by Brendon Netto, "For a footballer to make the most of his talent he must push himself beyond his limits and aspire to a higher standard. That's why many today, including those among the very best like Cristiano Ronaldo, are turning to personal trainers to help them excel."[17]

Achieving your desired life destiny is at least as important, if not more than, as Cristiano, Ighalo, LeBron, and Steph achieving theirs. Invest in yourself and your future with personalized coaching.

Coaching the fully integrated model of the A-attitudes of leadership and the iLEAD change processes and leveraging both subjective and objective measures to gauge progress and make necessary adjustments is especially important in year one. It is such a steep climb to initiate your journey that doing everything you can to sustain it through the first year is a critical success factor to make your destiny happen. Having an expert coach guide and support you through the first twelve months is prudent. After that, be aware that slowly veering off track to your desired destiny, like drifting into bad health habits, can happen and will negatively affect your quality of life and your well-being over time. Just like having regular checkups with your doctor is a good idea for your health, it is also important to have checkups with your coach on your personal transformation and life plan activation.

---

17   Brendon Netto, "From Cristiano Ronaldo to Odion Ighalo—Footballers Depend on Personal Trainers to Be Their Best," Sport 360, March 30, 2020, https://revamp-en.sport360.com/article/football/342969/from-cristiano-ronaldo-to-odion-ighalo-footballers-depend-on-personal-trainers-to-be-their-best.

SECTION 7
CLOSE AND CALL TO ACTION

Destiny Development Delta Model for Transformational Success

CHAPTER 28

CALL TO ACTION

Three decades ago, I envisioned my desired destiny and established my life plan. I developed the A-attitudes of leadership model to solidify my transformation and strengthen the holistic balance and personal well-being that I needed to support my life plan. I created the iLEAD change model as the defined road map to make my life plan a reality. I then refined and integrated them both to form the Destiny Development Delta model for transformational success.

The Destiny Development Delta model drives personal transformation that is leveraged to control one's destiny by following our defined methodology. It took me more than thirty years of personal trial and error while activating my life plan to create and refine the model and its related support processes and tools. But you don't have to wait thirty years. You can access the model that will transform your life now. Remember, it's your life, and you only get one, so start your transformation journey today to pursue the life and legacy that you desire.

Thank you for selecting the Destiny Development Delta model, and congratulations on embarking on the first step to make your destiny happen!

SECTION 8

ABOUT THE AUTHOR AND DESTINY DEVELOPMENT DELTA LLC

Donzel A. Leggett is the founder and principal of Destiny Development Delta LLC. He is an outspoken thought leader, an accomplished public speaker, an author, and a podcaster. Donzel's passion is coaching, developing, and mentoring people all over the world, and his vision and mission are to transform lives so that every person has the opportunity and capability to take control of their life and make their destiny happen. He created the Destiny Development Delta model to do just that. Donzel is a believer in the idea that we must actively drive the future that we want; therefore, he not only invests his time in coaching and mentoring individuals but also in philanthropic interests to improve society and the world. Donzel serves in various leadership roles on several local, national, and global nonprofit boards and advisory councils. Prior to starting Destiny Development Delta LLC, Donzel completed a thirty-two-year career as a highly respected senior leader in corporate America, renowned for driving high levels of engagement, commitment, and breakthrough performance through inspiration as well as organizational and personal transformation on a global scale. Originally from Key West, Florida, Donzel holds both Bachelor and Master of Science degrees in industrial technology from Purdue University, where he was an Academic All-America and three time Academic All-Big Ten football player. He also holds an MBA from Nova Southeastern University. He and his wife, Tracy, split their time between their homes in Southwest Florida and Chicagoland and have four adult children: Donnie, Sierra, Joanell, and Gianna.

Destiny Development Delta LLC is a US-based international consultancy focused on executive leadership development, leveraging our proprietary models and methodology. We offer a range of coaching engagement solutions to best support you in your journey to achieve your desired destiny. To learn more or to contact us directly, please visit www.DestinyDevDelta.com.

www.ingramcontent.com/pod-product-compliance
Lightning Source LLC
LaVergne TN
LVHW010451080925
820401LV00001B/8